Designing
Internet Home Pages
Made Simple

Second Edition

Lilian Hobbs

MADE SIMPLE
BOOKS

OXFORD AUCKLAND BOSTON JOHANNESBURG MELBOURNE NEW DELHI

Made Simple
An imprint of Butterworth-Heinemann
Linacre House, Jordan Hill, Oxford OX2 8DP
225 Wildwood Avenue, Woburn, MA 01801-2041
A division of Reed Educational and Professional Publishing Ltd

ℛ A member of the Reed Elsevier plc group

First edition published 1996
Second edition published 1999

British Library Cataloguing in Publication Data
A catalogue record for this book is available from the British Library

ISBN 0 7506 4476 1

Typeset by Lilian Hobbs, Southampton

Archtype, Bash Casual, Cotswold and Gravity fonts from Advanced Graphics Ltd
Icons designed by Sarah Ward © 1994
Transferred to digital print 2009
Printed and bound in Great Britain by CPI Antony Rowe, Chippenham and Eastbourne

Contents

Preface ix

1 The Web   1

The Web 2

What is HTML? 4

Web page elements 6

Planning your Web page 10

Structure of an HTML document 12

A simple first Web page 14

Viewing your page 16

Viewing source files 18

HTML editors 20

Summary 22

2 Working with text   23

Title 24

Plain text 26

Headings and text 28

Paragraphs 30

Highlighting text 32

Alignment 38

Preformatted text 40

Comments 42

Netscape Composer 44

FrontPage Express 46

Summary 48

3 More to do with text 49

Font size 50

Using colour 52

Lists 53

Lists without list tags 59

Lines 60

Tables 62

Tables in Netscape Composer 70

Tables in FrontPage Express 72

Style sheets 73

Summary 76

4 Graphics 77

Why use graphics 78

Including graphics 80

Text and spaces around a graphic 82

Alternative text 84

Transparent images 85

Fast graphic display 86

Using your photos 87

Graphics in tables 88

Graphics using HTML editors 91

Backgrounds 93

Summary 96

5 Links 97

Jumping 98

Multiple pages 100

Linking to other pages 102

Jumping with graphics 104

Image maps 106

Using image maps 107

Mapedit 109

Default style sheets 111

Summary 112

6 Frames and forms 113

Frames 114

Simple frame 116

Frames and targets 120

Nested frames 122

Forms 124

mailto: me! 125

Simple form 126

More form options 128

Form created by FrontPage Express 132

Summary 134

7 Active content 135

What is sound? 136

Including sound 138

Background sound 140

Including video 142

Scrolling message 144

Counters 146

Java 148

Javascript 154

Summary 158

8 Housekeeping   159

Installing your Web page 160

Uploading with Netscape 162

Good housekeeping 163

Uploading with Internet Explorer.......... 164

Opening your Web page 166

Home page 168

Telling the world.................................. 170

Meta 174

Space saving tips.................................. 176

Bringing it all together 177

Summary 178

Index   179

Preface

Almost all information on the Internet is held on Web pages, written in HyperText Markup Language — HTML. This book aims to show you how, using a few simple HTML commands, you can create good looking Internet pages that include both text and graphics. Now you can leave something behind on the Internet to tell other 'surfers' about yourself.

This book has been written to appeal to anyone who is new to the subject of HTML. Each technique such as writing text, including a picture or drawing a line is discussed individually, thereby allowing the reader to learn one skill before progressing onto another or only learn those techniques that are of value to them.

Alternatively, this book will serve as a handy reference to anyone who knows HTML but needs an easy-to-read reminder on the instructions required to implement a certain feature. It covers versions up to the current latest, HTML 4.0.

The first chapter introduces you to the Internet pages and the factors to consider when building your Web page. You will also be introduced to some of the tools that are available.

Over the next six chapters you will learn how to include text, graphics, sound and introduce some advanced techniques like jumping to other pages and building forms so people can send you messages. There will also be a short introduction on how to include Java applets on your Web page or interact with your visitors using Javascript.

The final chapter explains how to install your Web page on the Internet and register it with Internet search engines.

Lilian Hobbs

1 The Web

The Web 2

What is HTML? 4

Web page elements 6

Planning your Web page 10

Structure of an HTML document 12

A simple first Web page 14

Viewing your page 16

Viewing source files 18

HTML editors 20

Summary 22

The Web

The World Wide Web, commonly known as the Web, is one of the fastest growing areas on the Internet. It grew from a project in 1989 at CERN in Switzerland. The goal was to devise a way to share information over the Internet and look at what it has evolved into!

The Web is growing from a place where you could find information to a major place for commerce. In a few years, the Web has evolved from static, simple pages to highly sophisticated sites where you can buy goods and services safely. New companies have emerged which only do business over the Web, like the bookseller www.amazon.com.

Constructing a Web page is straightforward and once it is installed, it's there for the millions of Internet users to see. For a company, it is a tremendous marketing and new business opportunity, and for the home user — welcome to your biggest audience ever.

Information on the World Wide Web is held on Web pages. The first page is usually referred to as the **home page** and it is from here, that all pages are referenced. A personal Web page can contain absolutely anything that you like, but most service providers insist on no commercial advertising.

Just as a house has an address, so does every page on the Internet. This address is called a **URL** (Uniform Resource Locator) and using

Take note

Personal users wanting to connect to the Internet will need a modem, the faster the better, a browser to display the Web pages and a service provider who provides the connection. (Read *The Internet Made Simple* for more about connecting to the Internet.) Designing and writing Web pages, can be done off-line — without connecting to the Internet — thus saving you hefty telephone bills.

it, anyone can access your Web page. The precise naming scheme for your Web page can be advised by your Web administrator or service provider. Typically, they take the form of organization address and then an identifier. For example, the author's home page with service provider Claranet can be found at *http://home.clara.net/lmhobbs* where *home.clara.net* defines the Claranet site and *lmhobbs* is the page on that site.

The final component worthy of mention is the Web browser which is required to view Web pages. Although a number are available, the two in most common use are Netscape Navigator and Microsoft Internet Explorer. Which browser you use is a matter of personal preference and the level of HTML it supports (see next page).

Below is shown an example of a Web site displayed using Netscape.

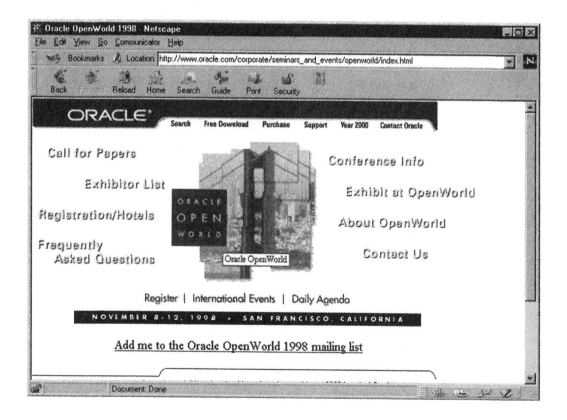

What is HTML?

Web pages are written using a system called **HTML** (HyperText Markup Language), which is continually evolving to meet the growing demands of the Internet. This book concentrates on how to create Web pages using HTML. Java and JavaScript are also becoming very popular and in a subsequent chapter we will see how to include Java applets and JavaScript code in our HTML documents.

Although HTML is used to create the page we see in the browser, it doesn't have to be hand-crafted as shown in this book. There are a number of editors available, such as Microsoft Front Page or Netscape Composer which create HTML documents. Using this approach should not be considered as cheating, rather a cost-effective use of your valuable time.

When surfing the Web, you may come across pages which say that this page is best viewed with a specific version of Netscape or Internet Explorer. If you do ever include any special HTML commands which only work on a certain browser, it is courteous to include this message. Several of these HTML statements will be illustrated in later chapters.

Another point worth remembering is that Web browsers often display information slightly differently, so don't be surprised if your page looks different on someone else's system.

So what is HTML? It's a mark-up system that comprises of **tags**, where a tag is an instruction contained within angle brackets, e.g.

Tip

If you want for ideas for using HTML, take a look at somebody else's Web page to see how they did it. Web browsers permit you to see the HTML used to create the Web page. In Netscape, use the command View – Page Source; in Internet Explorer 4.0, the command is View – Source.

<HTML> is a tag that defines the start of a HTML document. The vast majority of tags also have a closing tag, e.g. </HTML> defines the end of the document. HTML is constantly evolving, with new tags and extra facilities being added regularly. The current version — and the one which is the focus of this book — is 4.0.

Below is a sample of some of the HTML used to construct the author's Web page. Don't be put off by all these tags. When you have finished reading this book, it will all make sense! An important point to remember is that it is the tags which control the final appearance — not how you type the text in, so you can use indents and line breaks wherever you need to, to make the code easier to read.

```
<HTML>
<TITLE>Dr. Lilian Hobbs </TITLE>
<H1 >Home Page for Dr. Lilian Hobbs </H1>

<UL TYPE=circle>
    <LI> <A HREF="#books"> Books I have Written </A>
    <LI> <A HREF="#you"> Tell me about <I>Yourself </I> </A>
</UL>

<H2> <A NAME="books"> Books I Have Written </A> </H2>
Several years ago I had my first book published.
<P>
If you have ever thought that it is difficult to get books published, think
about writing non-fiction. The only problem is, you are unlikely to be able
to give up the day job!<P>
<ADDRESS>
    Dr. Lilian Hobbs <BR>
    Hampshire, UK
     <P>
        <A NAME="you">
        If you would like to send me mail click on my name
        <A HREF="mailto:lmhobbs@clara.net">Dr. Lilian Hobbs </A>
    <P>
    Page last modified: 24th May, 1998
</ADDRESS>
</HTML>
```

Web page elements

You probably have some idea of what you would like to include on your Web site, but if you are new to the Web, explore a little and see what is possible to achieve. There are examples throughout this book, but here are a few sites worth visiting.

- http://www.oracle.com – shows layout and frame usage;

- http://www.bbc.co.uk – demonstrates use of multiple pages;

- http://www.novaspace.com – excellent graphics;

- http://www.royal-and-sunalliance.com – user interaction.

If you are only creating personal pages, remember, that provided you have the space, you too can construct Web pages like these!

So what can you put on a Web page? A very simple page need only include text and this is a good place to start to familiarise yourself with HTML before moving onto more complex options.

Text

The British Astronomical Association only uses text, but nevertheless their pages are still informative, and very quick to display!

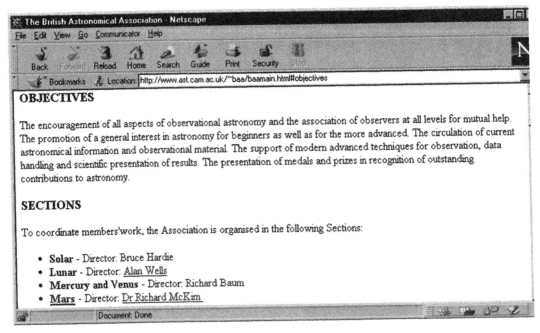

Graphics and Image Maps

A Web page of just text is not very exciting, so it's far more likely that you will want to include pictures. These pictures could be there just for information, like the ones at NASA showing pictures taken from the latest space mission or a personal site could contain family, holiday or wedding shots.

A common use for a graphic, is as a jump point to another Web page. The picture is used instead of words to describe where to go, or in conjunction with words. If the pointer changes to a hand when it is over a picture, it means that clicking on it will take you to that Web page or a different location within the current document. Pictures are fun to use but it is always good practice to include some text so that people can be sure what clicking on the picture will give them. Also, bear in mind that not everyone waits for the picture to display, and some people turn off image-loading altogether.

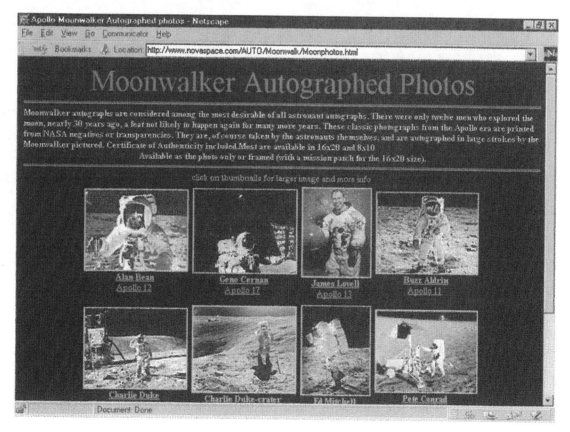

Forms

Whether you are a business or an individual, once your page is on the Web, it's nice to know who has read it or to get some feedback from visitors. This can be done through a form where they can respond to questions. You often meet forms at a commercial sites, such as the one shown below for a car insurance quote. But forms are for everyone, not just companies trying to sell you something — you will be surprised at who you will meet. The author has made contact with people from around the world, thanks to a form.

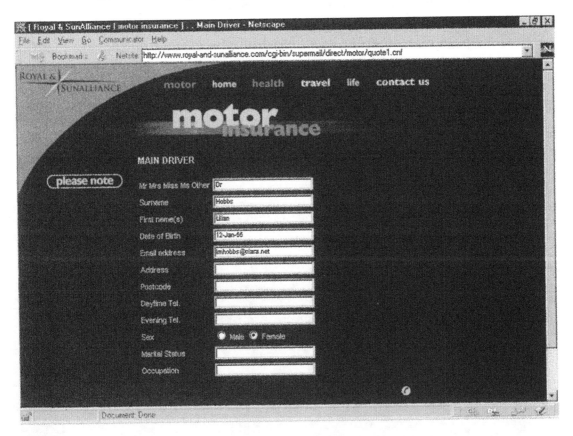

Frames

Frames are now being used on many Web sites. They have become so popular because they enable you to split your page into several areas, displaying different information in each area on the page. Take the following example from the *Performance Bicycle* site. This makes use of frames within the catalogue section to display a list of the components on the left-hand side, whilst saving the main area for textual and graphical information. By clicking on say *Helmets*, the left frame box will change to display all the helmets they sell. You can then click on a specific helmet to obtain more detailed information in the main window, while still maintaining a list of the all the helmets sold in the left frame box.

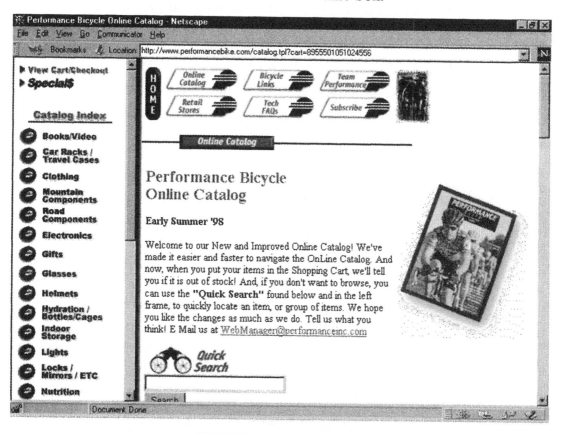

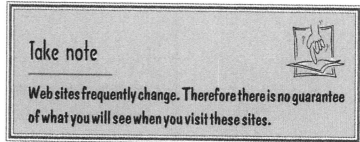

Take note

Web sites frequently change. Therefore there is no guarantee of what you will see when you visit these sites.

Planning your Web page

Now is the big moment, what do you want to include on your Web page? Why have you decided to announce yourself to the world? Is there something you want to tell everyone? How do you want to present your organisation to the world. It's entirely up to you what to include, but to give you some ideas:

- Tell us about your organization;

- Pictures, which could be of yourself or your products;

- Video of your product, a promotional trailer;

- A form where people can reply to questions you ask;

- Multiple pages to split the information into specific areas;

- Java applets to display promotional advertisements;

- Split the page into multiple framed areas;

- Use Javascript to perform more complex tasks;

- On a personal page tell us about your work or the hobbies you participate in. This is a good place to include links to other sites related to your hobby.

The first step is to decide what you want to include on the Web pages. This should involve drafting out on paper how each page will look, rather like the example on the facing page.

It is not uncommon for a commercial organisation to employ a graphic artist to design the look of the Web site because the task ahead is not that different to producing a leaflet or poster for a marketing campaign.

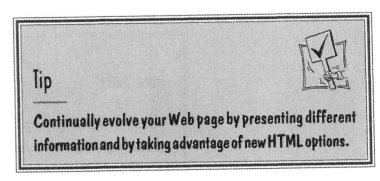

Tip

Continually evolve your Web page by presenting different information and by taking advantage of new HTML options.

Home Page for Dr. Lilian Hobbs

Frame 1

IMAGE MAP

- My Job
- My Spare Time
- Southampton Astro-nomical Society
- Babylon 5
- Pictures of me
- Tell me about yourself

```
Welcome Message
```

My Picture

| JAVA applet moving across the screen |

— Next Page

My Spare Time

My job keeps me very busy but I try to keep fit riding my mountain bike. It's a Cannondale full suspension model complete with mud guards and a cycle computer. Of course, I always wear a cycle helmet.

Southampton Astronomical Society

Table of programme

Babylon 5

B5 Logo   I am also a great fan of that excellent show Babylon 5

Tell me about yourself

Name:_____   Email:_____

o Female o Male

Why did you visit this site: o Curious o Accident o Recommended

Comments:

Structure of an HTML document

HTML is a simple language to learn and use. It is written using tags, where a tag is an instruction enclosed within < > (angle brackets). For example, the instruction to start a document is **<HTML>**. Tagged text is normally terminated with the same tag, but with a forward-slash. Therefore, the closing tag in this example is **</HTML>**.

The HTML document can be constructed using any editor such as Notepad or Wordpad. When the document is saved, it should have a file extension of .htm or .html.

HTML tags can be nested, therefore you could begin by using the tag to define a table and then within the table tags include HTML to format text or create a bulleted list. Another feature of the HTML language is that many tags have extra qualifiers, defined within the tags to describe the information they should display.

There are three tags which define the structure of the HTML document. The **<HTML>** tag is mandatory and defines the start and end of the document. The **<HEAD>** and **<BODY>** tags are optional, but should be used as they help to define the structure.

<HTML>

This tag defines the start of the HTML document and is always on the first line. The end of the document is defined by the **</HTML>** tag.

<HEAD>

The **<HEAD>** tag is used to define the header portion of the HTML document. Items such as the document title and the style of the document may be specified here. Keywords for search engines (see page 170) are also written here. Apart from the title, nothing written in the HEAD section is visible on the Web page. The section is located at the beginning of the document and must be terminated with a **</HEAD>** tag.

<BODY>

The **<BODY>** and **</BODY>** tags enclose the code which produces the visible Web page. Options within the <BODY> tag can be used to describe the characteristics of the Web page, such as background colour or the colour of text. A background image can also be defined within this tag.

Shown below is the typical framework for an HTML document comprising of the <HEAD> and <BODY> sections with some sample tags.

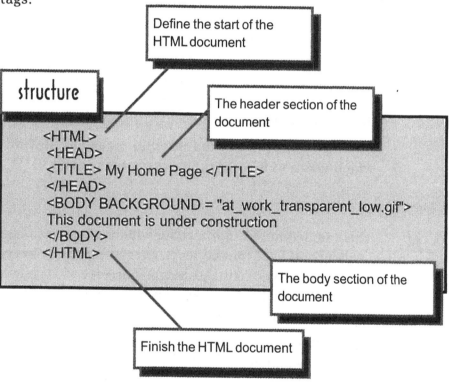

Define the start of the HTML document

structure

The header section of the document

```
<HTML>
<HEAD>
<TITLE> My Home Page </TITLE>
</HEAD>
<BODY BACKGROUND = "at_work_transparent_low.gif">
This document is under construction
</BODY>
</HTML>
```

The body section of the document

Finish the HTML document

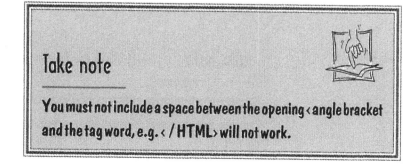

Take note

You must not include a space between the opening ‹ angle bracket and the tag word, e.g. ‹ / HTML› will not work.

A simple first Web page

Let's begin by creating a very simple first Web page which will contain simply your name in large bold letters. All the examples shown here, will be created using nothing more than the Windows Notepad, however, you can use any text editor to create them. This is not a very exciting first page, because its purpose is to introduce you to using the tags in the HTML language. The two used here are:

- <HTML>
- <H1>

Before starting to create your Web site it is a good idea to create a new folder or a directory to store all the components of your home page. It is also worth considering creating sub-folders for the other components such as pictures, Java applets and retired HTML documents that you may decide to archive.

Now select your favourite text editor such as the Windows Notepad which can be found in the Accessories group.

<H1>

This tag define the top heading which is why it is called H1. H for heading and 1 for the top level. Everything that you type after <H1> will be displayed as a heading. Therefore it is very important to specify the </H1> tag when you have finished writing the heading and this rule applies to every tag that has a closing tag.

Follow the numbered steps opposite to build your first Internet home page and see how it will look.

Take note

You can use your favourite word-processor instead of Notepad, if you prefer, but you must save the files as text, and with the .HTM extension.

14

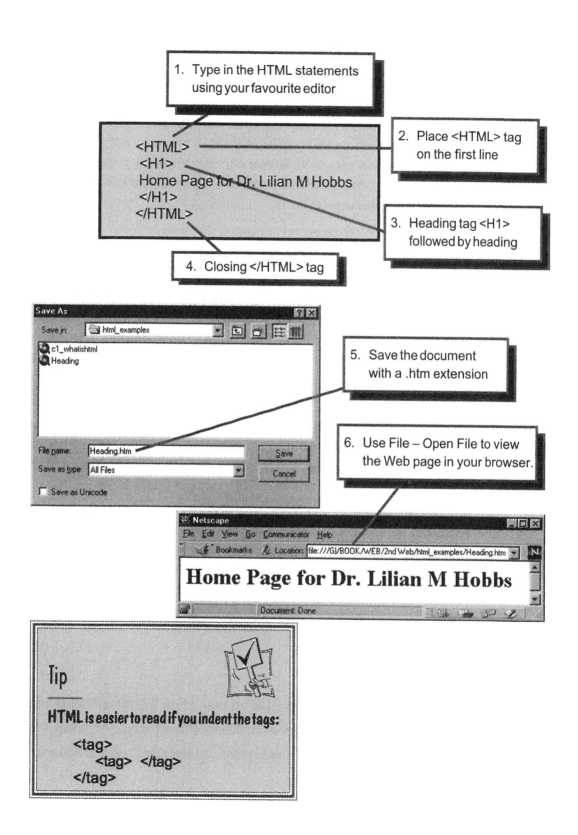

1. Type in the HTML statements using your favourite editor

```
<HTML>
  <H1>
  Home Page for Dr. Lilian M Hobbs
  </H1>
</HTML>
```

2. Place <HTML> tag on the first line

3. Heading tag <H1> followed by heading

4. Closing </HTML> tag

5. Save the document with a .htm extension

6. Use File – Open File to view the Web page in your browser.

Home Page for Dr. Lilian M Hobbs

Tip

HTML is easier to read if you indent the tags:

```
<tag>
    <tag>  </tag>
</tag>
```

15

Viewing your page

You have just written your first Web page, now it is time to see how it looks. Viewing is a simple process and the good news is, you don't have to be connected to the Internet. This not only can save you money, but also means that you can see how the page looks before it is installed onto the Web. After all, make a mistake and everyone on the Web can see it!

Viewing the Web page is achieved by using your Web browser. Every browser is different, but they all provide an option to open an HTML file, in Netscape it is on the **File** menu.

Take a look at your Web page, is it what you expected? The first time it probably isn't quite want you wanted. This is not a problem! No one ever gets it right first time, in fact most people have to make several changes. Typically a heading or graphic may be in the wrong place or you don't like the look and feel of the page. Making it look right takes a little time and is half the fun of creating Web pages.

As we progress through this book some of the tasks may seem rather complex. In this situation, you may prefer to use one of the many tools that are available to construct the page, instead of creating it manually.

Another important point to remember is that once an HTML document is on the Internet, it should be kept up to date. It is very easy to forget it, so make sure that Web page maintenance is included as part of your routine system administration.

Take note

Your Web browser may be set up to connect to an Internet site when it first starts. Therefore when you start the browser offline, it may appear to hang trying to make the connection. If this happens, just press the Stop icon. Now you can specify the file to display.

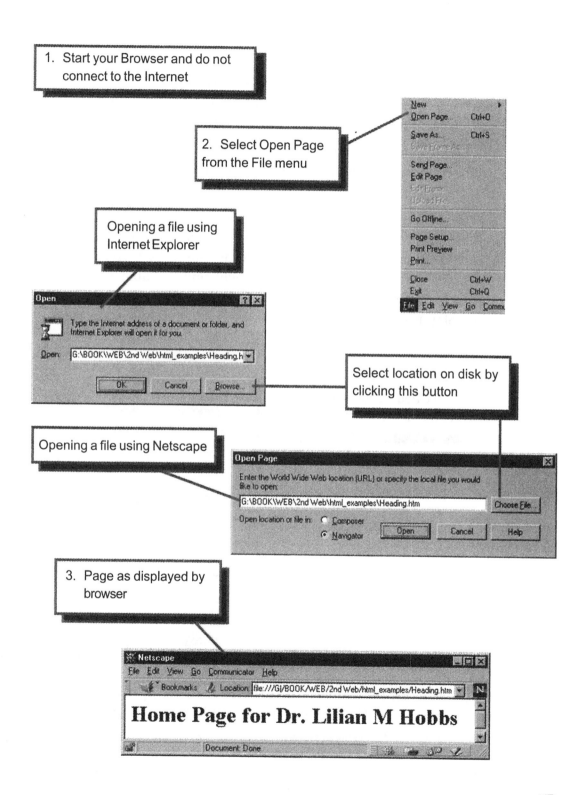

1. Start your Browser and do not connect to the Internet

2. Select Open Page from the File menu

New
Open Page...   Ctrl+O

Save As...   Ctrl+S
Save Frame As...

Send Page...
Edit Page
Edit Frame
Upload File...

Go Offline...

Page Setup...
Print Preview
Print...

Close   Ctrl+W
Exit   Ctrl+Q

File Edit View Go Commu

Opening a file using Internet Explorer

Open   ? X

Type the Internet address of a document or folder, and Internet Explorer will open it for you.

Open: G:\BOOK\WEB\2nd Web\html_examples\Heading.h ▼

OK   Cancel   Browse...

Select location on disk by clicking this button

Opening a file using Netscape

Open Page   X

Enter the World Wide Web location (URL) or specify the local file you would like to open:

G:\BOOK\WEB\2nd Web\html_examples\Heading.htm   Choose File

Open location or file in: ○ Composer   Open   Cancel   Help
                            ● Navigator

3. Page as displayed by browser

Netscape   _ □ X

File Edit View Go Communicator Help

Bookmarks   Location: file:///G|/BOOK/WEB/2nd Web/html_examples/Heading.htm ▼   N

Home Page for Dr. Lilian M Hobbs

Document: Done

Viewing source files

While surfing you will probably come across pages and will say to yourself, *'how did they do that?'* Well the good news is they can't keep it a secret, because you can view the source HTML from your Web browser and even save it for future reference.

One point to bear in mind is that this HTML may be specific to the original author's browser. Therefore, there is no guarantee it will work on your system.

The technique described here applies to any Web page browser. All that may differ is the terminology used to open and view the HTML. Another important point to consider is that if the Web page is using frames (see Chapter 6), then you will only be able to see all the HTML source code if your browser provides the capability to display frame sources as well as the HTML source.

Select **Page Source** in Netscape or **Source** in Internet Explorer

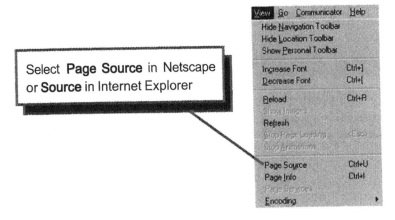

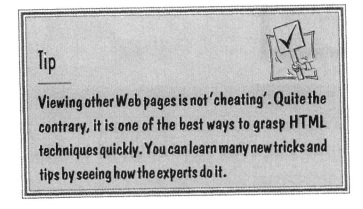

Tip

Viewing other Web pages is not 'cheating'. Quite the contrary, it is one of the best ways to grasp HTML techniques quickly. You can learn many new tricks and tips by seeing how the experts do it.

GSM MoU Association - Microsoft Internet Explorer

File Edit View Go Favorites Help

Back | Forward | Stop | Refresh | Home | Search | Favorites | Print | Font | Mail

Address http://www.gsmworld.com/gsminfo/cou_ca.htm

| Home | News | Assoc. | History | GSMInfo |

Canada

Microcell Telecom Inc

| Network | Roaming | Services | Coverage | Web Site |

Back to GSMInfo index

Site Content and Data Copyright: GSM MoU Association and its members.
This web site is developed and managed by Coversoft Ltd on behalf of the GSM MoU Association.

Last updated May 18, 1998

cou_ca - Notepad

File Edit Search Help

```
<!-- Start of Buttons -->
<NOBR><A HREF="net_cami.htm"><IMG BORDER=0 SRC="../images/net.gif" WIDTH=68 HEIGHT=28  AI
<BR>
<!-- End of Buttons -->
</TABLE>
<!-- Page Footer -->
<TABLE CELLPADDING=0 CELLSPACING=0 BORDER=0 WIDTH=100%>
<TR>
<TD WIDTH=127><IMG SRC="../images/border.gif" WIDTH=127 HEIGHT=1 BORDER=0></TD><TD ALI
<BR>
<FONT FACE="Verdana, Arial, Helvetica" SIZE=2 COLOR="#000000">
<A HREF="gsminfo.htm">Back to GSMInfo index</A>
</FONT>
<BR><BR>
<TR>
<FONT FACE="Verdana, Arial, Helvetica" SIZE=1 COLOR="#000000">
Site Content and Data Copyright: <A HREF="mailto:marketing@gsmmou.org">GSM MoU Association</A> and
<BR>
This web site is developed and managed by <A HREF="mailto:gsmworld@coversoft.com">Coversoft Ltd</A> or
<P>
<B>Last updated May 18, 1998</B>
</FONT>
</TD>
</TR>
</TABLE>
</BODY>
</HTML>
```

HTML tags

HTML editors

There is an alternative to writing the HTML yourself and that is to use a software product to create your Web page. Although HTML is fairly easy to write, if you don't feel up to the task ahead, especially if you are trying to create something that uses a number of HTML tags, then an editor will do the job quickly and easily. There are a number available on the Internet, if the one you select isn't freeware, please ensure the continued development of the product, by paying the appropriate fee. The products used in this book are Front Page Express, supplied with Internet Explorer 4.0, and Composer, which is part of the Netscape Gold packages and the Communicator suite.

Using editors to create Web pages, should not be seen as 'cheating'! They provide a useful helping hand, especially when you are first getting started. Once the software has created the initial document, you can then edit it by hand and add extra features that may not be available in the software.

Editors are also useful when you have something complex to create. For example, creating a table is tricky due to the number of tags required to define each cell in the table. So in this instance, why not use the software and open your existing HTML document. Edit it to add the table and then save it again. You could then continue to maintain this document manually in the future.

There are many editors available, some are self-contained and others integrate with word processing software like Microsoft Word, Ami Pro and Wordperfect. When they integrate directly with a product, you have the added advantage of not needing to learn a new tool, only a few new commands to use the options.

Of course, if you are in the business of professional Web publishing then you can use software like Microsoft Front Page, the full-featured version of Front Page Express.

Here we can see the same Web page being created using Netscape Composer and Front Page Express. A document created by one editor, will not always display correctly in another, although the HTML generated will result in the browser output being the same.

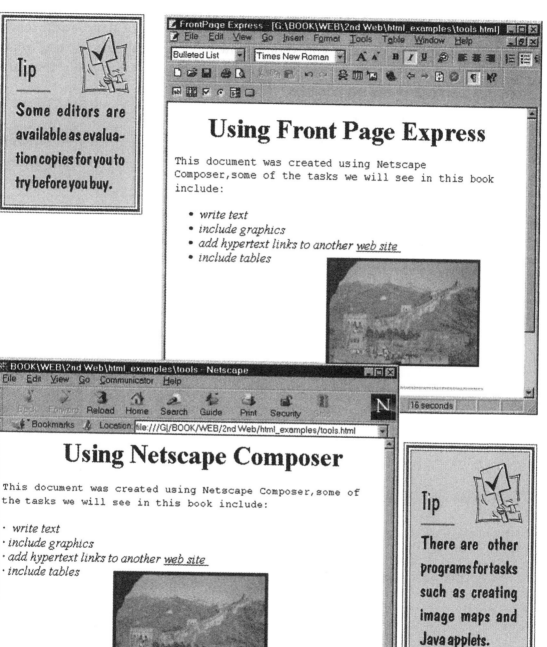

Using Front Page Express

This document was created using Netscape Composer, some of the tasks we will see in this book include:

- *write text*
- *include graphics*
- *add hypertext links to another web site*
- *include tables*

Using Netscape Composer

This document was created using Netscape Composer, some of the tasks we will see in this book include:

· *write text*
· *include graphics*
· *add hypertext links to another web site*
· *include tables*

Summary

At the end of this chapter, although you may not have learnt many of the HTML tags, you should now have an understanding of what is involved in creating a Web page and the basic skills that are required before you start writing HTML.

Some useful tasks to complete include:

- ❏ Collect all the information that is to be presented on your Web page, this includes the text to be displayed, photographs, images and video.

- ❏ Start to draft out how this information is to be presented.

- ❏ Decide which text editor will be used and create a Web page comprising of the basic structure.

- ❏ Familiarise yourself with the procedure for displaying the Web page in your browser.

2 Working with text

Title 24

Plain text 26

Headings and text 28

Paragraphs 30

Highlighting text 32

Alignment 38

Preformatted text 40

Comments 42

Netscape Composer 44

FrontPage Express 46

Summary 48

Title

After the <HTML> and <HEAD> tags, the next item that needs to be included on a Web page is a title which requires the tag **<TITLE>**. Include this tag on every document because:

- it appears as the title in the window;
- when someone saves your Web page, the title will appear in their bookmark list if they are using Netscape — Internet Explorer users will be asked if they want to use the title;
- anyone using a Web search engine will see this name as the title of your Web page.

The title can be anything. For a personal page, your name or nickname is the obvious choice. If the page is being designed for commercial use, set a new title for every page, as visitors may bookmark several pages and it is annoying to find that every page has the same title.

The definition of the title is completed by using the tag </TITLE>.

The title on the Paramount Web site is 'Welcome to Paramount Pictures'

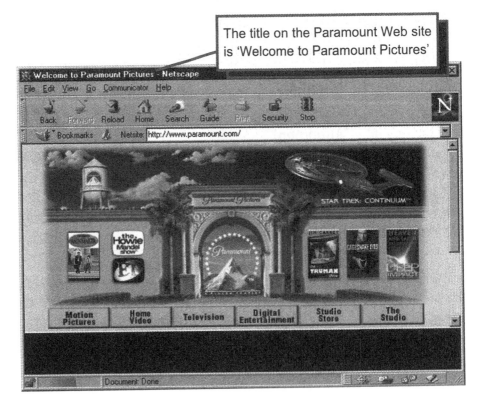

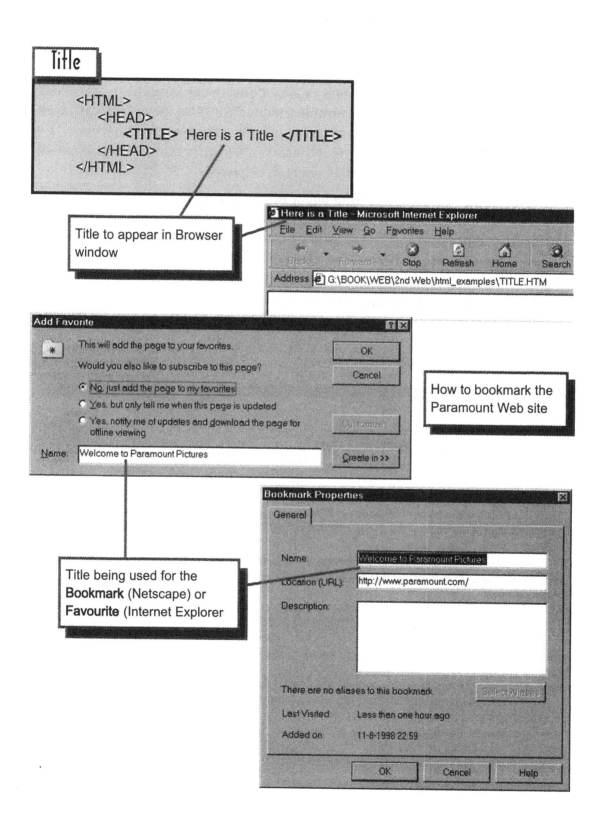

Title

```
<HTML>
   <HEAD>
      <TITLE> Here is a Title </TITLE>
   </HEAD>
</HTML>
```

Title to appear in Browser window

Here is a Title - Microsoft Internet Explorer

File Edit View Go Favorites Help

Back   Forward   Stop   Refresh   Home   Search

Address G:\BOOK\WEB\2nd Web\html_examples\TITLE.HTM

Add Favorite

This will add the page to your favorites.

Would you also like to subscribe to this page?

- No, just add the page to my favorites
- Yes, but only tell me when this page is updated
- Yes, notify me of updates and download the page for offline viewing

Name: Welcome to Paramount Pictures

OK

Cancel

Customize

Create in >>

How to bookmark the Paramount Web site

Title being used for the **Bookmark** (Netscape) or **Favourite** (Internet Explorer

Bookmark Properties

General

Name: Welcome to Paramount Pictures

Location (URL): http://www.paramount.com/

Description:

There are no aliases to this bookmark.   Select Aliases

Last Visited: Less than one hour ago

Added on: 11-8-1998 22:59

OK   Cancel   Help

25

Plain text

Although most Web pages make extensive use of graphics, they still have to include considerable amounts of text. Including text in an HTML document is easy, and needs no formatting, because the browser is responsible for that task. When plain text is being included, it is the only time that a tag is not required.

It can be very tempting when building a Web site to include many graphics and only have a small percentage of text. However, one very important point to remember is that the Web can be slow returning information, even if you have a very fast connection to the Internet. If the site takes too long to display, the visitor may decide to abandon your site and move onto another. Graphics are slower to download than text – a page of text may be less than a kilobyte, but a single graphic may require 30 kilobytes or more.

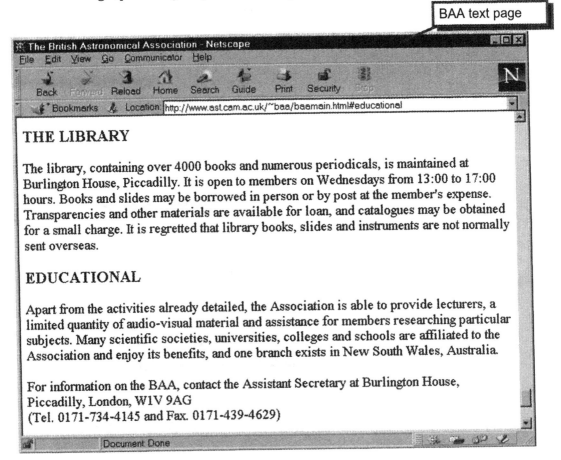

BAA text page

THE LIBRARY

The library, containing over 4000 books and numerous periodicals, is maintained at Burlington House, Piccadilly. It is open to members on Wednesdays from 13:00 to 17:00 hours. Books and slides may be borrowed in person or by post at the member's expense. Transparencies and other materials are available for loan, and catalogues may be obtained for a small charge. It is regretted that library books, slides and instruments are not normally sent overseas.

EDUCATIONAL

Apart from the activities already detailed, the Association is able to provide lecturers, a limited quantity of audio-visual material and assistance for members researching particular subjects. Many scientific societies, universities, colleges and schools are affiliated to the Association and enjoy its benefits, and one branch exists in New South Wales, Australia.

For information on the BAA, contact the Assistant Secretary at Burlington House, Piccadilly, London, W1V 9AG
(Tel. 0171-734-4145 and Fax. 0171-439-4629)

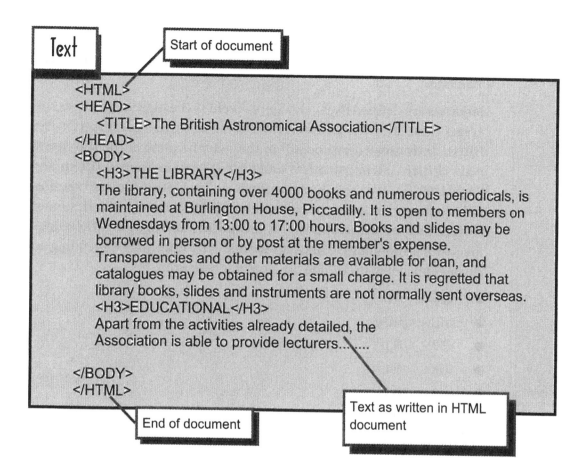

Referring to this example from the British Astronomical Association Web site, the text is written in the HTML document as per normal text writing. When the page is displayed, the browser automatically formats the text and generates new lines when required. Whenever the browser window is changed in size, the text is automatically adjusted to fit in the available window. Note how the browser displays a ragged edge. Shortly we will see how we can align the text and create our own line breaks.

Headings and text

One of the first steps we completed when designing our Web page was to group the subject matter together and put it under different headings.

Headings are defined by level, where level 1 is the highest and uses the largest font, 2 the next and so forth. Referring to our example from the British Astronomical Association, the main heading at the top of the page, *British Astronomical Association* is level 1. Each of the topics would then be level 2 such as Contents. A description for each section is then placed under a level 3 heading. HTML permits a maximum of 6 levels, but you will probably not use more than 3 or 4. All of these tags have a corresponding closing tag such as </H1> and </H2> depending on the heading being used. The six heading tags are:

- <H1> </H1>
- <H2> </H2>
- <H3> </H3>
- <H4> </H4>
- <H5> </H5>
- <H6> </H6>

To specify the heading text, simply write the text after the heading tag and then finish it with the terminating tag.

Headings are extremely useful and a useful technique which we will see later is how to jump to a specific heading in a document.

If the default font and size is unsuitable then it can be changed using a style sheet (see page 73), provided that your browser supports this feature.

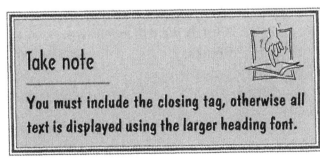

Take note

You must include the closing tag, otherwise all text is displayed using the larger heading font.

Headings and text

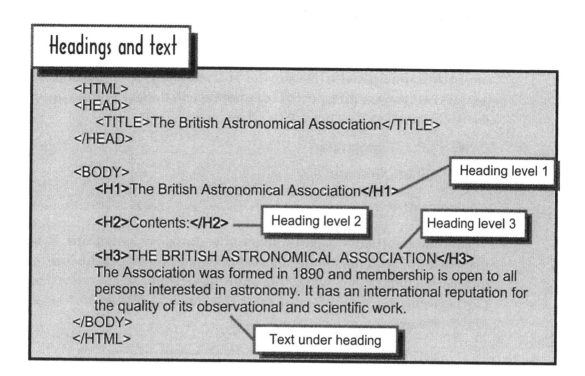

```
<HTML>
<HEAD>
    <TITLE>The British Astronomical Association</TITLE>
</HEAD>

<BODY>
    <H1>The British Astronomical Association</H1>

    <H2>Contents:</H2>

    <H3>THE BRITISH ASTRONOMICAL ASSOCIATION</H3>
    The Association was formed in 1890 and membership is open to all
    persons interested in astronomy. It has an international reputation for
    the quality of its observational and scientific work.
</BODY>
</HTML>
```

Heading level 1

Heading level 2

Heading level 3

Text under heading

How the browser displays
the HTML document

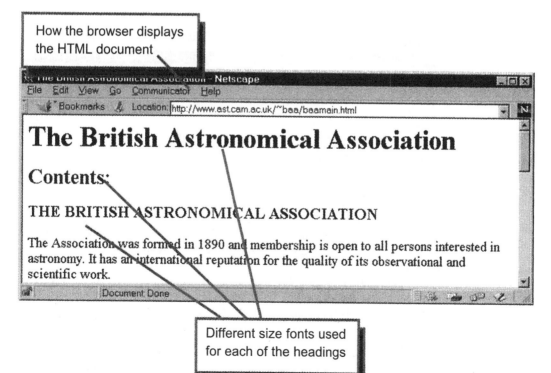

Different size fonts used
for each of the headings

Paragraphs

One of the problems with the browser automatically reformatting the text, is that the resulting output may not be what you require. There are two important tags to include when writing text.

- <P>   Paragraph;
-
  New line.

<P>

This is the tag that is used to define the start of a paragraph. It is placed at the beginning of each paragraph and causes a blank line to be inserted before the text written after the **<P>** tag. This is one of the few tags that has the option of using the closing **</P>** tag and most HTML authors do not use the </P> tag.

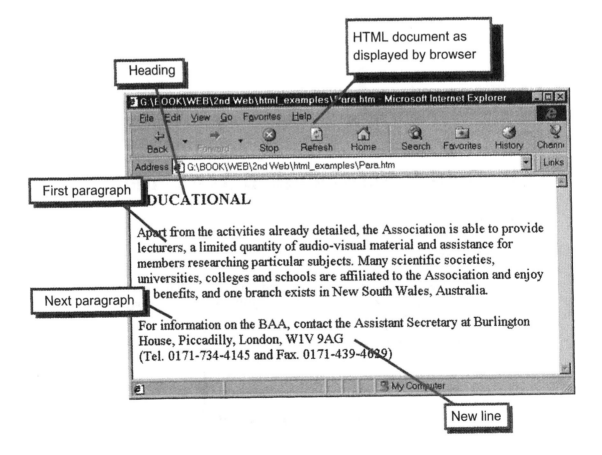

Sometimes you may want to start a new line without creating a blank line above it. This is achieved using the **
** tag which starts text on the next line.

When these tags are used, it is not uncommon to include them at the start or end of the text. This can result in difficulty in identifying where a new paragraph or line may start when you are editing your HTML code. It is suggested that the <BR> and <P> tags reside on their own line. This will also help the author appreciate how the Web page might look in the browser.

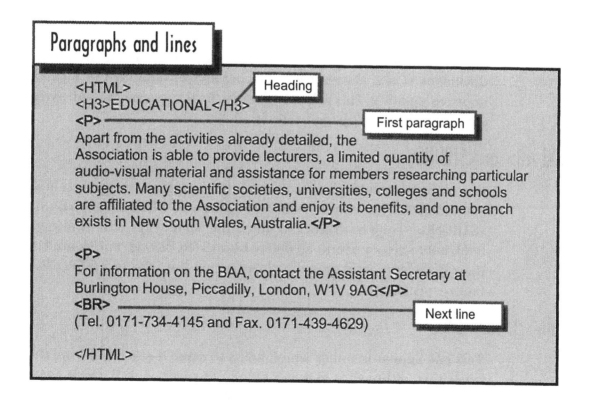

Paragraphs and lines

```
<HTML>                              Heading
<H3>EDUCATIONAL</H3>
<P>                                      First paragraph
Apart from the activities already detailed, the
Association is able to provide lecturers, a limited quantity of
audio-visual material and assistance for members researching particular
subjects. Many scientific societies, universities, colleges and schools
are affiliated to the Association and enjoy its benefits, and one branch
exists in New South Wales, Australia.</P>

<P>
For information on the BAA, contact the Assistant Secretary at
Burlington House, Piccadilly, London, W1V 9AG</P>
<BR>                                      Next line
(Tel. 0171-734-4145 and Fax. 0171-439-4629)

</HTML>
```

Highlighting text

Sometimes, certain words or phrases in text need to be brought to the readers' attention. HTML provides the ability to:

- **embolden** a word
- display in *italics*
- <u>underline</u> words
- cause words to blink

Text is highlighted by inserting the appropriate tag before the word or phrase to be highlighted, with the equivalent 'off' tag at the end of the text, to close it. It is very important to remember to use the closing tag. Without it, text will remain highlighted!

Since these tags are embedded within the text, reading the HTML document is not always easy. Placing spaces around the tags to improve legibility. This will not affect the final appearance as all extra spaces are ignored by the browser.

Bold <B> or <STRONG>

One of the best methods to make text stand out from normal text is to embolden it. This can be achieved using one of two tags, **<B>** or **<STRONG>**. They both work in much the same way – <B> is always bold, but in theory users can define how <STRONG> is represented in their browsers – and must be closed using the **</B>** or **</STRONG>** tags respectively.

Italic <I> or <EM>

Text can appear in italics which helps to make it stand out from the other text, although it may not stand out quite as well. Once again there is a choice of two tags, **<I>** or **<EM>** (emphasis, user-definable) and they must be closed using the **</I>** and **</EM>** tags respectively.

Underline <U>

Text can be underlined using the <U> tag and closed with the </U> tag.

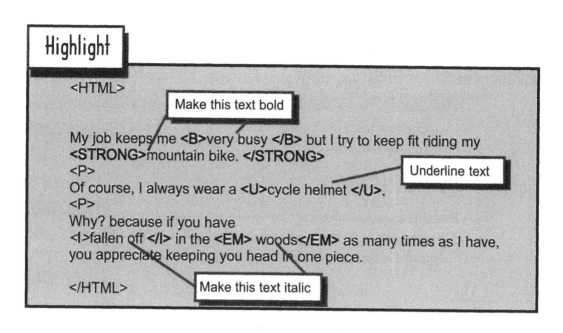

```
<HTML>
```

Make this text bold

```
My job keeps me <B>very busy </B> but I try to keep fit riding my
<STRONG>mountain bike. </STRONG>
<P>
Of course, I always wear a <U>cycle helmet </U>.
<P>
Why? because if you have
<I>fallen off </I> in the <EM> woods</EM> as many times as I have,
you appreciate keeping you head in one piece.

</HTML>
```

Underline text

Make this text italic

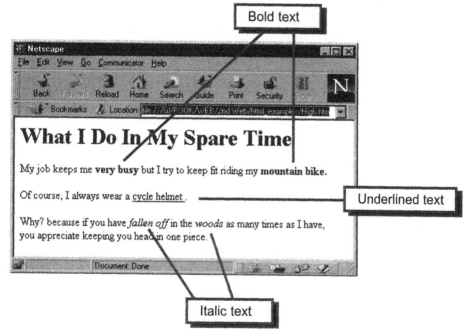

Bold text

Underlined text

Italic text

33

Blinking <BLINK> (Netscape Only)

The selected text will blink. However, be advised that not all browsers support this tag. Don't forgot to terminate the blinking text using the closing tag **</BLINK>**.

Quotation <Q> and <CITE>

If text is a quotation which needs to stand out from the rest of the text. This can be achieved using the **<Q>** and **<CITE>** tags and is closed using the **</Q>** and **</CITE>** tags respectively.

Sample <SAMP>

The sample output tag can prove to be very useful. It allows you to include any text, such as the output from a program. To format the text inside the tag, tags such as **
** must be included to generate a new line.

Subscript <SUB>

Sometimes you may want to include scientific notification on your Web page, which can be achieved using the **_{** tag. For example, to display the chemical symbol for water, H_2O. DOn't forget to close with the **}** tag.

Superscript <SUP>

The **<SUP>** tag is the opposite of the <SUB> tag because it raises the text, rather than lower it. Therefore this is the tag to use for displaying scientific notification, as in the example opposite, or for names, such as Scottish ones like McKenzie. Close with the </SUP> tag.

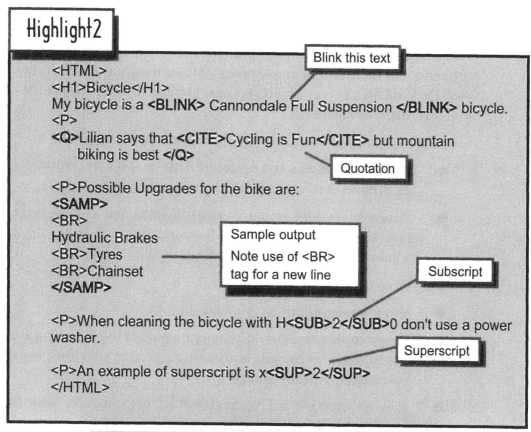

Highlight2

```
<HTML>
<H1>Bicycle</H1>
My bicycle is a <BLINK> Cannondale Full Suspension </BLINK> bicycle.
<P>
<Q>Lilian says that <CITE>Cycling is Fun</CITE> but mountain
   biking is best </Q>

<P>Possible Upgrades for the bike are:
<SAMP>
<BR>
Hydraulic Brakes
<BR>Tyres
<BR>Chainset
</SAMP>

<P>When cleaning the bicycle with H<SUB>2</SUB>0 don't use a power
washer.

<P>An example of superscript is x<SUP>2</SUP>
</HTML>
```

- Blink this text
- Quotation
- Sample output / Note use of <BR> tag for a new line
- Subscript
- Superscript

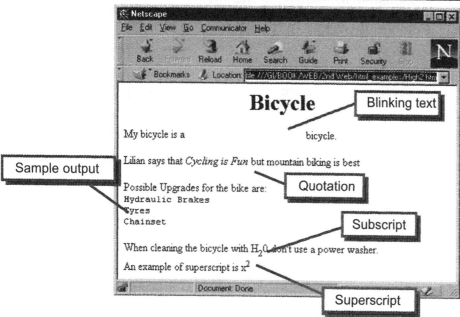

Address

Many Web pages, usually at the bottom of the page, contains some reference information. For consistency, this information can be styled with the <ADDRESS> tag, which sets text in italic in a slightly smaller font size than normal text.

Some of the things you can include in an address section are:

- *Date the page was last updated.* This enables the reader to determine how accurate the information on the page is.

- *Your name with a contact email address.* We will see later how someone can click on text and this will bring up a window so that they can send you email.

- Your *location* or department.

- *Other contributors* to the Web site

- Commercial sites should consider which of the following are appropriate; *copyright notice, registered trademarks, legal disclaimer, privacy policy*

- How to *contact the Webmaster* or organisation who is responsible for managing the site.

- Number of *visitors* to the site

<ADDRESS>

The address starts with **<ADDRESS>** and is closed with the **</ADDRESS>** tag. If several lines are needed, you must insert the <BR> tag to move to a new line and use the <P> tag to leave a blank line.

All the formatting tags such as <B> and <U> can be used inside the address tag along with the tags to include graphics or links to other Web sites. See how in the example, the clause ALIGN= is used to place the text in the centre of the page and the <P> tag was used to create a new text block.

The suggested contents for the page footer don't have to be included within the <ADDRESS> tag. Many sites, display this information using ordinary tags and there is nothing wrong with this approach.

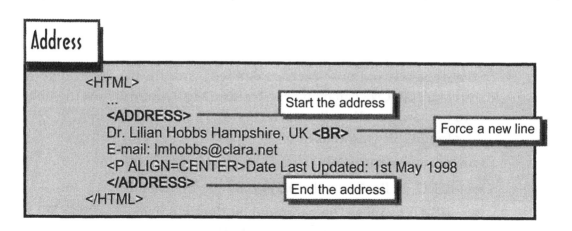

```
<HTML>
    ...
    <ADDRESS>
    Dr. Lilian Hobbs Hampshire, UK <BR>
    E-mail: lmhobbs@clara.net
    <P ALIGN=CENTER>Date Last Updated: 1st May 1998
    </ADDRESS>
</HTML>
```

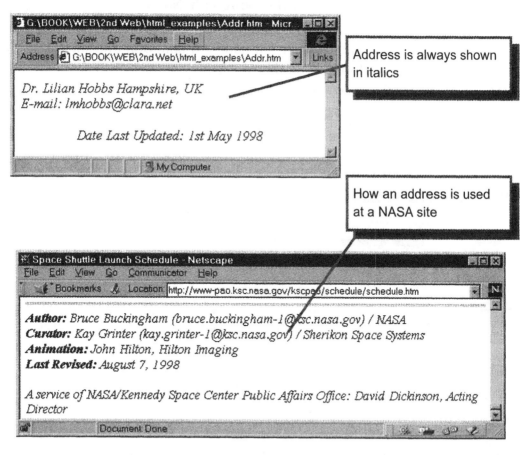

Address is always shown in italics

How an address is used at a NASA site

Alignment

Some tags have options which are defined inside the tag. For example, the clause **ALIGN=** can be placed inside a tag to control how the text is to be positioned, as illustrated below.

<Tag ALIGN= keyword >

where the keywords are:

- **LEFT**   Positions the paragraph on the left side.
- **RIGHT**   Aligns the paragraph at the right end.
- **CENTER** Centres the paragraph. Note American spelling.
- **JUSTIFY** Attempts to adjust the paragraph so that every line ends on the same right-hand column. Don't be surprised if it doesn't look completely justified, because the browser only makes a best attempt.

Throughout this book the **ALIGN=** clause will be seen in numerous examples. It can be used within many tags to format paragraphs, headings and graphics.

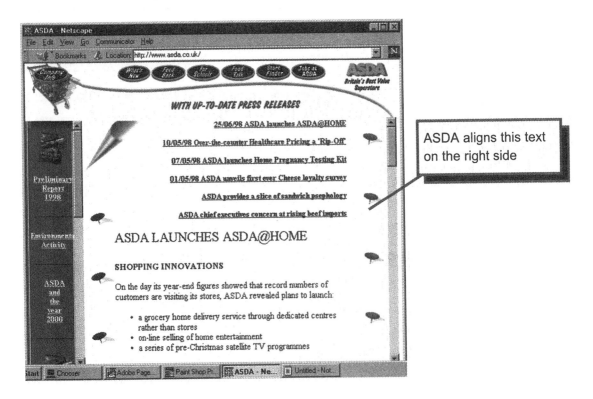

ASDA aligns this text on the right side

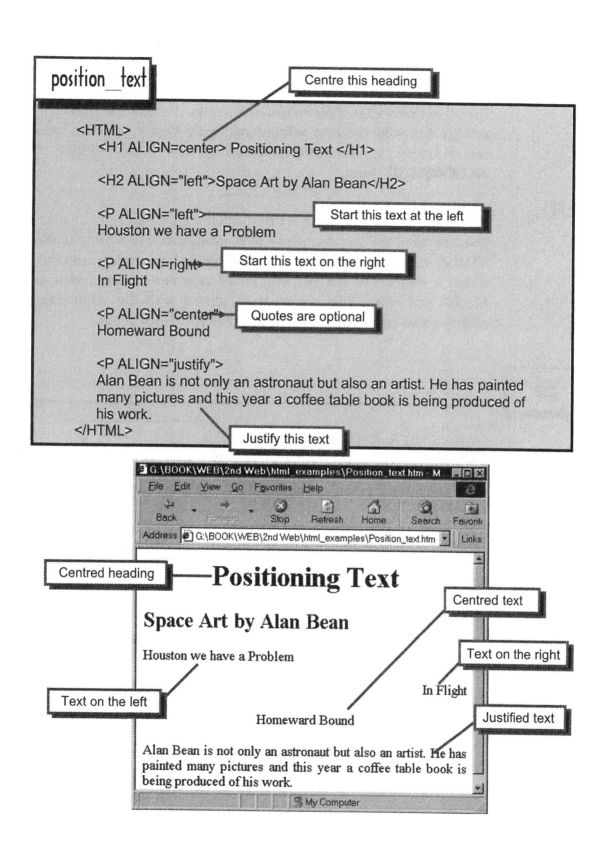

position_text

Centre this heading

```
<HTML>
    <H1 ALIGN=center> Positioning Text </H1>

    <H2 ALIGN="left">Space Art by Alan Bean</H2>

    <P ALIGN="left">
    Houston we have a Problem

    <P ALIGN=right>
    In Flight

    <P ALIGN="center">
    Homeward Bound

    <P ALIGN="justify">
    Alan Bean is not only an astronaut but also an artist. He has painted
    many pictures and this year a coffee table book is being produced of
    his work.
</HTML>
```

Start this text at the left

Start this text on the right

Quotes are optional

Justify this text

G:\BOOK\WEB\2nd Web\html_examples\Position_text.htm - M

File Edit View Go Favorites Help

Back   Forward   Stop   Refresh   Home   Search   Favorit

Address G:\BOOK\WEB\2nd Web\html_examples\Position_text.htm   Links

Centred heading

Positioning Text

Space Art by Alan Bean

Centred text

Houston we have a Problem

Text on the left

Text on the right

In Flight

Homeward Bound

Justified text

Alan Bean is not only an astronaut but also an artist. He has
painted many pictures and this year a coffee table book is
being produced of his work.

My Computer

39

Preformatted text

There are times when it is desirable to display the text exactly as it is written. Since the browser will automatically format your text, you can override the default behaviour by use of the **<PRE>** or **<BLOCKQUOTE>** tags.

<PRE>

This tag takes the text and displays it, exactly as it is written in the HTML document. This tag is useful when specific formatting is required, which is difficult to achieve with HTML tags and clauses, such as ALIGN= and <BR>. This tag must be closed with the </PRE> tag otherwise no subsequent formatting of any text will occur.

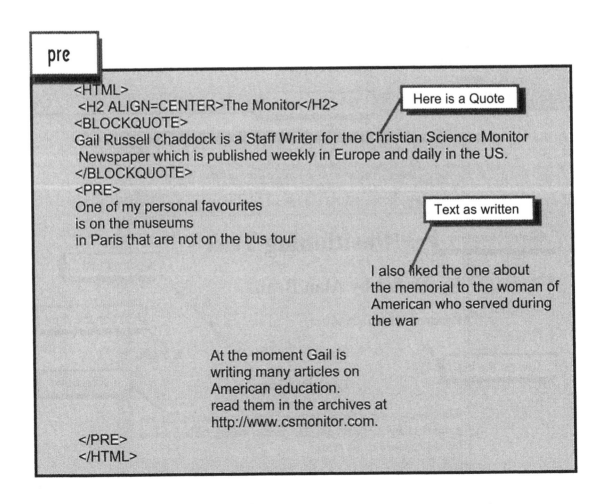

pre

```
<HTML>
 <H2 ALIGN=CENTER>The Monitor</H2>
<BLOCKQUOTE>
Gail Russell Chaddock is a Staff Writer for the Christian Science Monitor
 Newspaper which is published weekly in Europe and daily in the US.
</BLOCKQUOTE>
<PRE>
One of my personal favourites
is on the museums
in Paris that are not on the bus tour
```

Here is a Quote

Text as written

I also liked the one about
the memorial to the woman of
American who served during
the war

```
            At the moment Gail is
            writing many articles on
            American education.
            read them in the archives at
            http://www.csmonitor.com.

</PRE>
</HTML>
```

It is however suggested that the <PRE> tag is only used when absolutely necessary. If text is formatted automatically, the reader sees the entire width of the page. But with pre-formatted text, it is displayed exactly as it was entered in the HTML file, which means some information could be lost off the side of the display.

<BLOCKQUOTE>

The **<BLOCKQUOTE>** tag will automatically format the text, however, it is different because the text is automatically indented. Therefore this tag is extremely useful for making text stand out on the Web page. In the example below, you can see how the font is changed from the standard font in order to emphasize the text.

Blockquote, indented and emboldened

Netscape
File Edit View Go Communicator Help

Back Forward Reload Home Search Guide Print Security Stop

Bookmarks Location file:///G|/BOOK/WEB/2nd Web/html_examples/Pre.htm

The Monitor

Gail Russell Chaddock is a Staff Writer for the Christian Science Monitor Newspaper which is published weekly in Europe and daily in the US.

```
One of my personal favourites
is on the museums
in Paris that are not on the bus tour
```

Text as written in document

```
                                        I also liked the one about
                                        the memorial to the woman of
                                        American who served during
                                        the war
```

```
              At the moment Gail is
              writing many articles on
              American education.
              read them in the archives at
              http://www.csmonitor.com.
```

Document Done

Comments

It is extremely good practice to include comments in your Web documents, just as you would if you were writing a computer program. Unless the Web page is very simple, it will help you or anyone else in the future, understand what was written.

Useful comments to include are the author's name, and either the date the document was last changed or a revision history list. Normally authors only include the date the document was last changed, but HTML documents are becoming more complex, especially if, for example, Javascript or other advanced features are being used. The HTML document should then be considered a piece of programming code where comments are essential. Although it may seem obvious to you now what this document is doing, in a few months' time it might not make sense at all.

The <!—> tag is used to start the comment and <—> to close it. You can write as many comments as you like because they are invisible on the finished page. A comment can be placed anywhere on a line because the only time it can be viewed, is when the source for the page is requested.

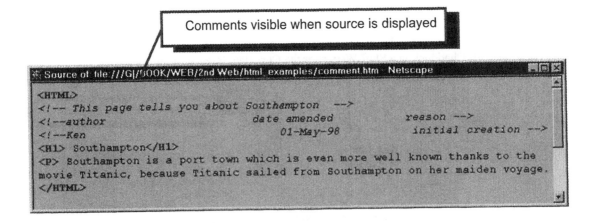

Comments visible when source is displayed

Source of file:///G|/BOOK/WEB/2nd Web/html_examples/comment.htm - Netscape

```
<HTML>
<!-- This page tells you about Southampton   -->
<!--author                    date amended        reason -->
<!--Ken                       01-May-98           initial creation -->
<H1> Southampton</H1>
<P> Southampton is a port town which is even more well known thanks to the
movie Titanic, because Titanic sailed from Southampton on her maiden voyage.
</HTML>
```

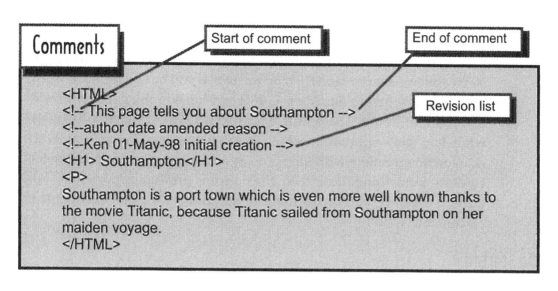

Comments

Start of comment

End of comment

```
<HTML>
<!-- This page tells you about Southampton -->
<!--author date amended reason -->
<!--Ken 01-May-98 initial creation -->
<H1> Southampton</H1>
<P>
Southampton is a port town which is even more well known thanks to
the movie Titanic, because Titanic sailed from Southampton on her
maiden voyage.
</HTML>
```

Revision list

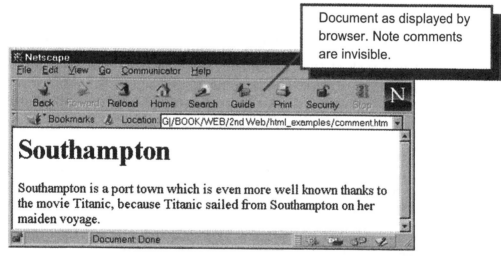

Document as displayed by browser. Note comments are invisible.

Southampton

Southampton is a port town which is even more well known thanks to the movie Titanic, because Titanic sailed from Southampton on her maiden voyage.

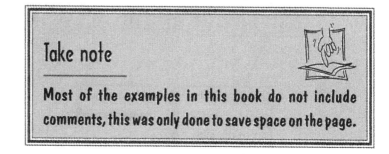

Take note

Most of the examples in this book do not include comments, this was only done to save space on the page.

Netscape Composer

Netscape Composer is an editor that comes with Netscape Communicator or Netscape Gold. It can be started directly from the Netscape browser or launched on its own. If you have ever used word processing software like Microsoft Word for Windows then you will feel quite at home. The editor uses the WYSIWYG (what you see is what you get) approach, which means that you create the Web document, complete with lines, tables and images just as you expect to see it, but behind the screen, the editor is producing normal HTML code. Therefore you never need to see the HTML that creates the document.

Getting started

When Netscape Composer first launches, take some time to explore and understand the options available from the icons at the top of the screen, because this is what you will need to create your document.

If you look at the screenshot below, you can see all the different options available. For example, clicking on the **H.Line** icon will draw a horizontal line. To select the type of text such as heading, text or list, select it from the drop-down list on the left.

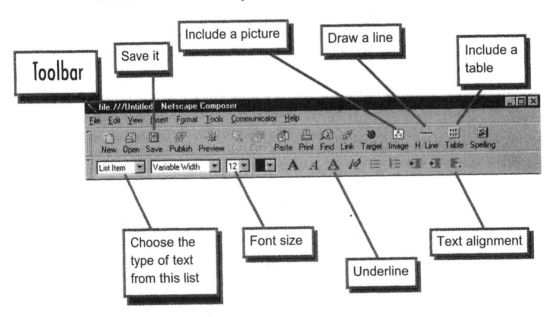

Once you are familiar with the options, it's time to create your first document. By default you are presented with a blank screen. Type your text and format it, either by selecting a style from the drop down list, such as a heading or text, or by choosing the font size, font and whether the text is to be bolded and how it is to be aligned. Although this may sound a lot to do, if you are use to using a word processor, it will be familiar. Repeat this process for all the text that you want on the page. In the example below we can see text using the Heading1 and normal format.

When you are entering text, it is very easy to make a typing mistake. No one wants to publish a Web page with spelling mistakes, but it is very easy to do unless you run the source file through a spelling checker. Netscape Composer provides no excuses because you can click on the *spelling* icon at anytime to check for mistakes. Do remember, however, that it won't pick up words which are wrong rather than misspelt, e.g. 'you' instead of 'your'.

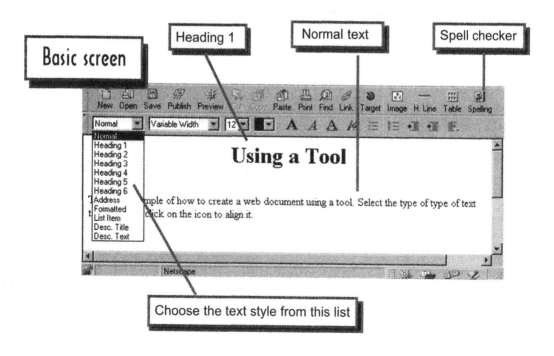

FrontPage Express

Microsoft have a very good application for designing Web pages, called FrontPage, but for the average home user, its cost is probably too high. However, do not despair, when you install Microsoft Internet Explorer 4, one of the options you can select is a cut-down version called FrontPage Express. It is easy to use and will enable you to generate very nice Web pages.

Getting started

When you launch the editor, it looks, at first glance, very similar to Netscape Composer. Using the icons shown here you can select a heading, a font, specify the font size or include a graphic or table.

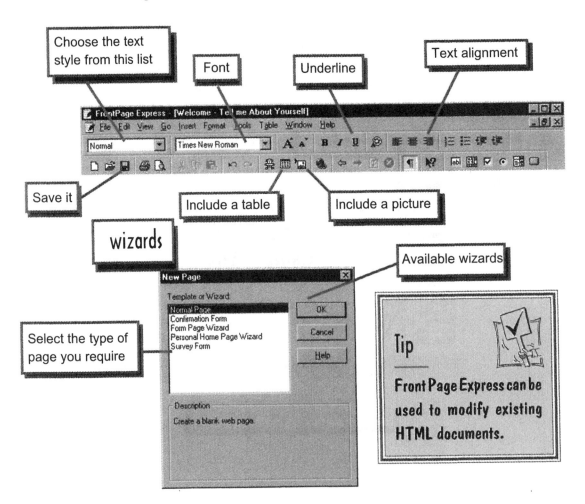

Choose the text style from this list

Font

Underline

Text alignment

Save it

Include a table

Include a picture

wizards

Available wizards

Select the type of page you require

Tip

Front Page Express can be used to modify existing HTML documents.

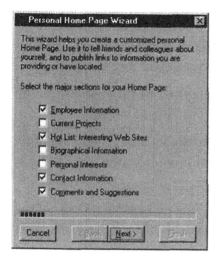

When you select a new page, the first prompt you see is which wizard you would like. If you select *Normal Page*, which is highlighted in the example then a blank page appears. But if you are not sure of what you want to include, then select one of the wizards. For example, choosing *Personal Home Page* will present you with these questions. If you remember, back in Chapter 1 we were presented with the dilemma of what we wanted to include on our Web site. Well now all we need to do is answer these questions and a rather nice Web page will appear for very little effort.

The page produced probably won't match your needs completely, but it is easy to modify the skeleton provided. For example, here we can:

- change the background colour from grey;

- add a picture;

- delete any bullets that are no longer required;

- change the text;

- include a table;

- add a hypertext link.

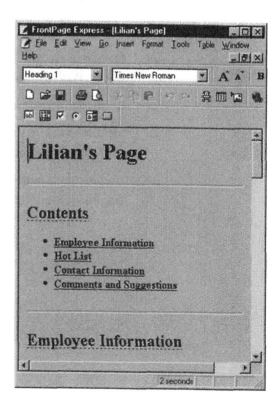

Summary

In this chapter we have seen many different techniques that we can use to include text on our Web page. Text is simple to include and unless formatting is required, doesn't even need any special tags.

Using the numerous options available, text can be aligned and highlighted and some browsers even allow your text to blink.

We can now start to practise good Web page design and include hidden comments with every document and standard reference information at the bottom of every page.

HTML doesn't have to be crafted by hand and we saw examples of two popular software products which can make the job of generating Web pages considerably easier.

Useful techniques to practise now include:

❑ experimenting with the different options for aligning text;

❑ using paragraphs;

❑ create a default template for comments which is included in every Web document you create;

❑ using different heading levels and try some nested headings;

❑ decide what reference information should be written at the bottom of every Web page;

❑ investigate whether any software products like FrontPage Express are available for your use.

3 More to do with text

Font size 50

Using colour 52

Lists 53

Lists without list tags 59

Lines 60

Tables 62

Tables in Netscape Composer 70

Tables in FrontPage Express 72

Style sheets 73

Summary 76

Font size

So far we have displayed text and seen how to emphasis it, but there is another tag available, **<FONT>** which allow us to specify the size of the font, its colour and the actual font. Changing these is another way of bringing text to the readers' attention.

<FONT>

The **<FONT>** tag changes the appearance of all following text until changed by another <FONT> tag, or the settings are restored to their defaults with the closing **</FONT>** tag.

Size=

The font can be displayed in a range of sizes ranging from 1 to 7, where 7 is the largest and 1 is the smallest. These size numbers bear no resemblance to the font sizes in word-processors. Alternatively, the font size can be increased or decreased by using the plus (+) or minus (–) sign and a value, e.g. **<FONT SIZE = + 2>**.

Color=

The colour of the text being displayed can be controlled by specifying this attribute. The value can be given in words or hexadecimal numbers — see page 52 for more details on how to use this.

Face=

The font can be specified using this attribute. Use this with care. If your readers don't have the font on their system, this will not work. The standard Windows fonts are a fairly safe bet.

Tip

If different styles are needed for headings, lists and text, use the ‹STYLE› tag – see page 70.

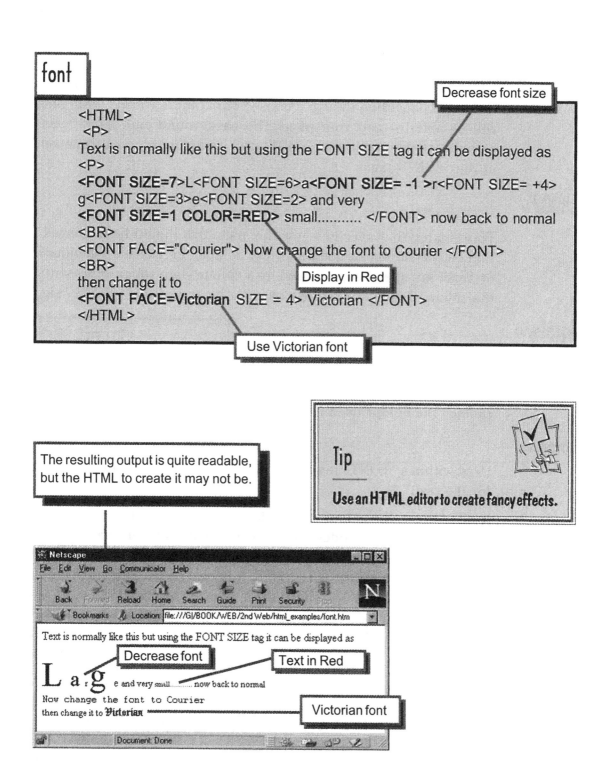

font

Decrease font size

```
<HTML>
<P>
Text is normally like this but using the FONT SIZE tag it can be displayed as
<P>
<FONT SIZE=7>L<FONT SIZE=6>a<FONT SIZE= -1 >r<FONT SIZE= +4>
g<FONT SIZE=3>e<FONT SIZE=2> and very
<FONT SIZE=1 COLOR=RED> small.......... </FONT> now back to normal
<BR>
<FONT FACE="Courier"> Now change the font to Courier </FONT>
<BR>
then change it to
<FONT FACE=Victorian SIZE = 4> Victorian </FONT>
</HTML>
```

Display in Red

Use Victorian font

The resulting output is quite readable, but the HTML to create it may not be.

Tip

Use an HTML editor to create fancy effects.

Netscape

File Edit View Go Communicator Help

Back Forward Reload Home Search Guide Print Security Stop

Bookmarks Location: file:///G|/BOOK/WEB/2nd Web/html_examples/font.htm

Text is normally like this but using the FONT SIZE tag it can be displayed as

Decrease font

Text in Red

L a r g e and very small.......... now back to normal

Now change the font to Courier

then change it to Victorian

Victorian font

Document: Done

Using colour

The use of coloured text or different background colours on a Web page, can totally change the look of what might be a drab Web site. One word of caution though, choose your colours wisely, or no one will be able to read your page! The background and default text colours are defined in the <BODY> tag. Text colour can also be set in the <FONT> tag.

<BODY>

This is a tag that specifies how the main text should be displayed. To control the background and text colour, the clauses **Bgcolour=** or **Text=** are specified, followed by a colour code which represents the colour. The text must be closed at the end with a </BODY> tag.

Bgcolor=

Specifies the background colour.

Text=

Defines the colour used for all text.

Take note

The tag uses the American spelling of 'color'.

Color=

Used within a <FONT> tag to specify the colour which must be used for the text.

In all of these, the colour is specified using a keyword such as "red", or using one of the codes shown below. This is a very basic list of colours, but it is possible to define a whole range of different ones. Unless a special colour is required, it is best to use the name "red" than its code "#FF0000". (Note the # sign at the start!)

Colour Codes

Black	#000000	Blue	#0000FF
Gray	#808080	Yellow	#FFFF00
White	#FFFFFF	Aqua	#00FFFF
Red	#FF0000	Magenta	#FF00FF
Green	#00FF00	Purple	#800080

Lists

Lists are used extensively on Web pages, because they are ideal for presenting options to the reader, such as in this example by the AA.

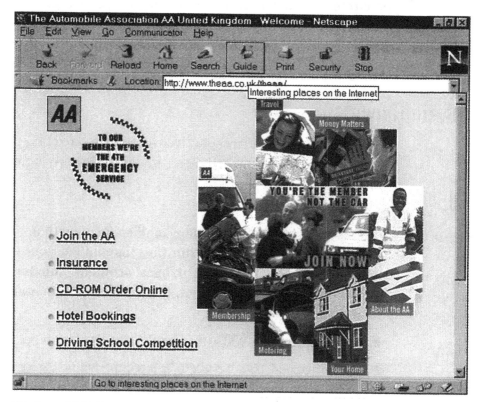

Within HTML, several different types of lists may be created, therefore the possibilities for their use is quite extensive.

In HTML the list options are:

- unnumbered with a bullet of your choice;
- numbered using your numbering scheme;
- definition list.

Several tags are needed to create a list of items. The first tag determines the type of list, such as numbered. Then each line in the list begins with the <LI> tag. Finally the list is concluded with the terminating tag for the list type.

Lists can also be created by using tables or paragraphs, which is sometimes more suitable than using these tags.

<UL> Unnumbered list

An unnumbered list with a bullet. The default bullet is a filled-in circle, but by adding **TYPE=** you can change it to a **square, disc** or **circle**. The list is terminated with a **</UL>** tag.

<LH> List header

Define the header for a list, closed with a **</LH>** tag.

<LI> List Entry

All entries in the list, irrespective of the type, are specified using the <LI> tag. The text is placed after the tag and there is no closing tag.

<OL> Numbered list

Creates a list of numbered items and is closed with a </OL> tag. The use of the **TYPE=** clause within the tag enables you to specify the numbering style. By default it uses ordinary numbers and starts with 1, but **A** generates letters, **I** large Roman numerals and **i** small Roman numerals.

- You can use **START=** to specify the first number in the list.
- An item can also be given a specific value using the **VALUE=** clause in the <LI> tag.
- The numbers can also be changed by including the clause **SKIP=** inside the <LI> tag.

<DL> Definition List

If a glossary is required, then this would be a good use for a Definition List. Start with the tag **<DL>**. Each term is defined using the **<DT>** tag and described using the **<DD>** tag. All of the tags must be closed with the appropriate **</DL>**, **</DT>** and **</DD>** tags.

An example of an unnumbered list: this page on the 1999 Solar Eclipse enables the reader to find out the chances of seeing the eclipse in their area.

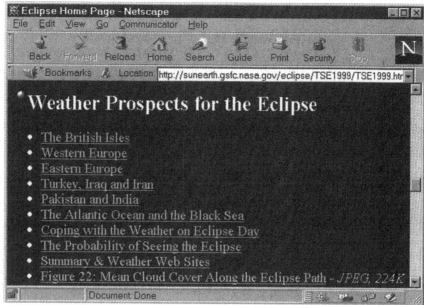

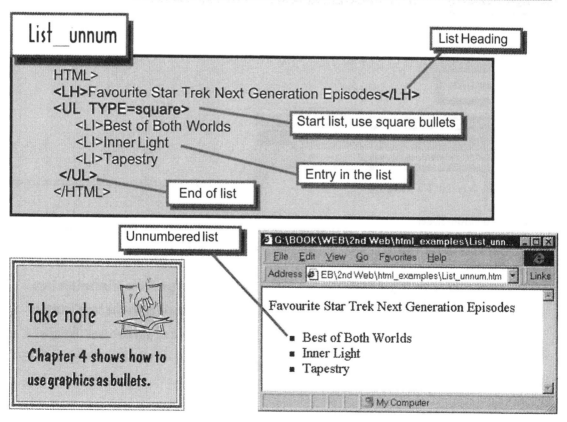

List_unnum

List Heading

```
HTML>
<LH>Favourite Star Trek Next Generation Episodes</LH>
<UL TYPE=square>
    <LI>Best of Both Worlds
    <LI>Inner Light
    <LI>Tapestry
</UL>
</HTML>
```

Start list, use square bullets

Entry in the list

End of list

Unnumbered list

Take note

Chapter 4 shows how to use graphics as bullets.

Ordered List

An ordered list can start with any value as per the example shown below. Any list can be indented and each list can have its own numbering scheme. Although the examples shown here use numbers, an ordered list could contains letters or roman numerals.

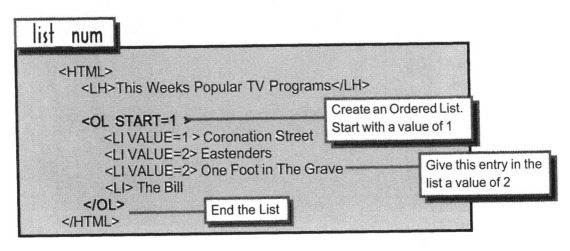

```
list_num

<HTML>
    <LH>This Weeks Popular TV Programs</LH>

    <OL START=1 >                          Create an Ordered List.
        <LI VALUE=1 > Coronation Street    Start with a value of 1
        <LI VALUE=2> Eastenders
        <LI VALUE=2> One Foot in The Grave    Give this entry in the
        <LI> The Bill                          list a value of 2
    </OL>            End the List
</HTML>
```

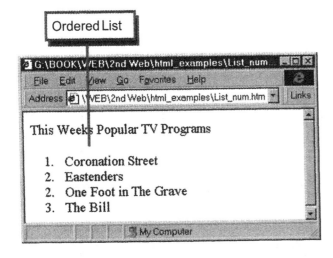

Ordered List

G:\BOOK\WEB\2nd Web\html_examples\List_num...

File Edit View Go Favorites Help

Address \\WEB\2nd Web\html_examples\List_num.htm ▼ | Links

This Weeks Popular TV Programs

1. Coronation Street
2. Eastenders
2. One Foot in The Grave
3. The Bill

My Computer

Tip

It's a good idea to indent the tags. This will make the code easier to read and will also look like a list.

56

Definition List

At first glance a definition list could be mistaken for a heading and indented text, where each block of text is placed in its own paragraph. The size of the font for the heading or text can be changed using the <FONT SIZE> tag so that it emulates the heading tag.

A nice example using a definition list can be found at the Sustrans site at http://www.sustrans.org.uk/ although at first glance one would think it is a bulleted list.

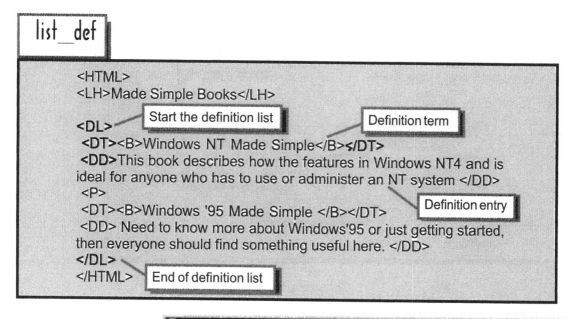

```
list_def

<HTML>
<LH>Made Simple Books</LH>

<DL>                 Start the definition list        Definition term
  <DT><B>Windows NT Made Simple</B></DT>
  <DD>This book describes how the features in Windows NT4 and is
ideal for anyone who has to use or administer an NT system </DD>
  <P>
  <DT><B>Windows '95 Made Simple </B></DT>      Definition entry
  <DD> Need to know more about Windows'95 or just getting started,
then everyone should find something useful here. </DD>
</DL>
</HTML>     End of definition list
```

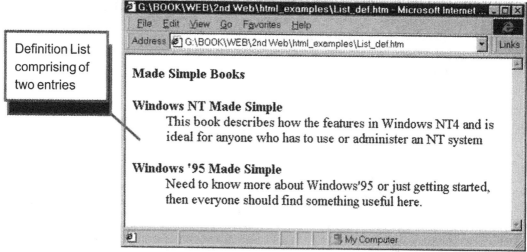

Definition List comprising of two entries

G:\BOOK\WEB\2nd Web\html_examples\List_def.htm - Microsoft Internet ...

File   Edit   View   Go   Favorites   Help

Address G:\BOOK\WEB\2nd Web\html_examples\List_def.htm   Links

Made Simple Books

Windows NT Made Simple
   This book describes how the features in Windows NT4 and is
   ideal for anyone who has to use or administer an NT system

Windows '95 Made Simple
   Need to know more about Windows'95 or just getting started,
   then everyone should find something useful here.

My Computer

Nested List

All of the lists described can also be nested as illustrated below. It is a very good idea to indent the tags according to their level in the list, then they will be easy to edit.

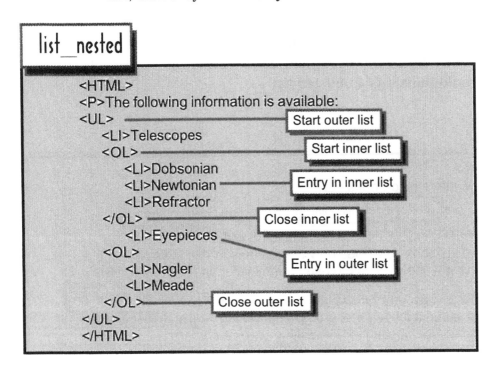

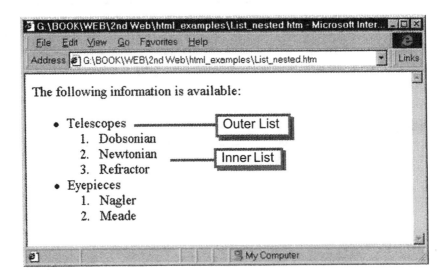

Lists without list tags

Lists do not have to be created using the tags just described. Here are some examples of Web sites that look at first glance, as though list tags are in use. However, if you review the source for these pages then you will see that other techniques have been used.

For example, these very nice lists on the Disability Net page, have been created using a table.

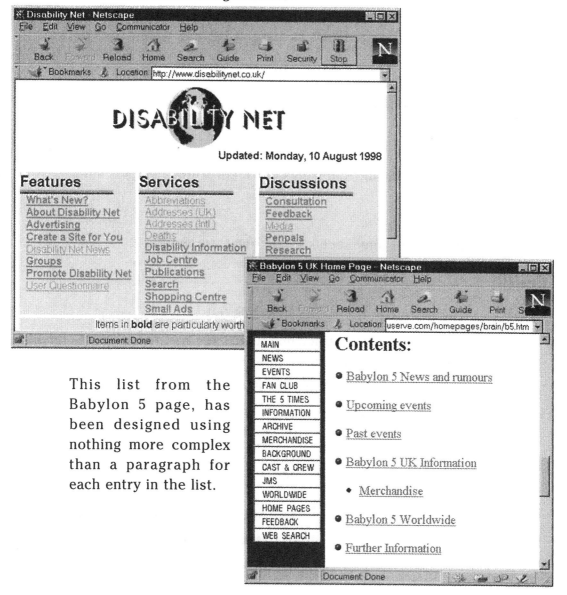

This list from the Babylon 5 page, has been designed using nothing more complex than a paragraph for each entry in the list.

Lines

If you have an HTML document with many different sections, you can draw a line between them, or anywhere in the page, using the tag **<HR>**.

<HR>

The tag is called <HR> because it stands for horizontal ruler. It has no closing tag. A simple **<HR>** generates a line across the page. But you can also specify within the tag the following parameters:

SIZE =

Size of the line

WIDTH=

Length of the line, in pixels or as a percentage of the window width.

ALIGN =

Position of line, such as **left**, **right** or **center**.

NOSHADE

Will fill in the line so that it stands out.

Therefore to draw a thick line that stretches across 75% of the page from the centre, the tag would be:

<HR SIZE=5 WIDTH=75% ALIGN=CENTER>

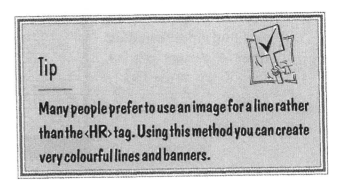

Tip

Many people prefer to use an image for a line rather than the <HR> tag. Using this method you can create very colourful lines and banners.

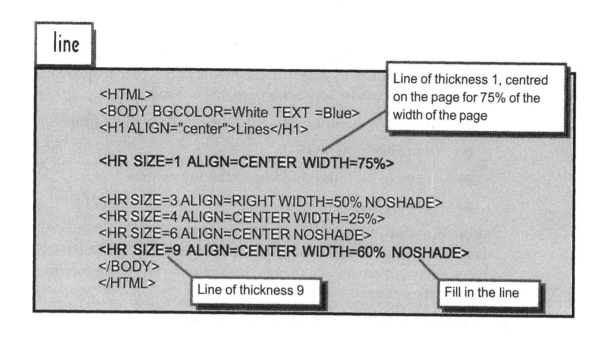

line

```
<HTML>
<BODY BGCOLOR=White TEXT =Blue>
<H1 ALIGN="center">Lines</H1>

<HR SIZE=1 ALIGN=CENTER WIDTH=75%>

<HR SIZE=3 ALIGN=RIGHT WIDTH=50% NOSHADE>
<HR SIZE=4 ALIGN=CENTER WIDTH=25%>
<HR SIZE=6 ALIGN=CENTER NOSHADE>
<HR SIZE=9 ALIGN=CENTER WIDTH=60% NOSHADE>
</BODY>
</HTML>
```

Line of thickness 1, centred on the page for 75% of the width of the page

Line of thickness 9

Fill in the line

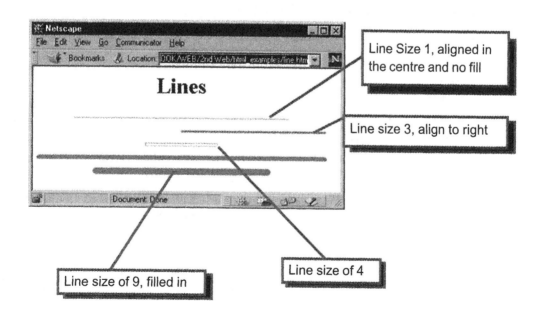

Line Size 1, aligned in the centre and no fill

Line size 3, align to right

Line size of 9, filled in

Line size of 4

Tables

One of the most commonly-used structures found on a Web page is a table. Tables are popular with Web designers because they provide a mechanism to layout text and graphics. There are many ways they can be used on a Web page, for instance:

- to display the programme for the meetings of a group;

- to include graphics;

- anything that needs to be written in columns;

- creating navigation areas.

When you think of a table, probably the first usage that comes to mind is to display simple columns of information, like the Web page shown below, which details the current episode of a TV show being aired in the different TV regions.

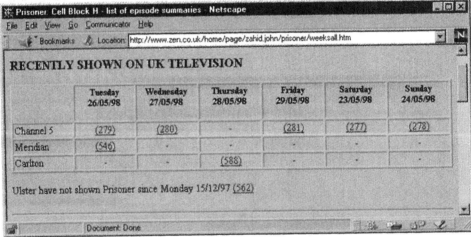

Another very common use for tables on a Web page is to organise text or graphics together (see the examples opposite).

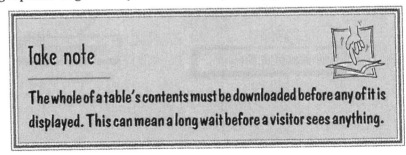

Take note

The whole of a table's contents must be downloaded before any of it is displayed. This can mean a long wait before a visitor sees anything.

Novagraphics (www.novaspace.com) uses
a table to display the pictures on sale.

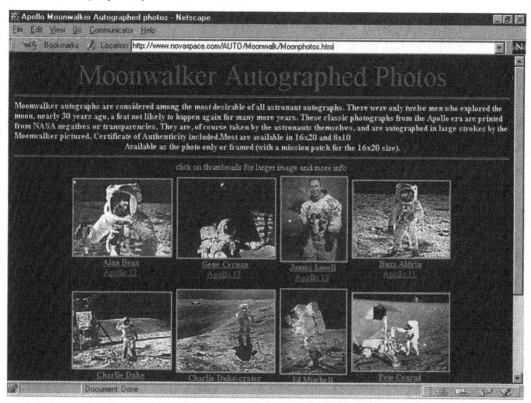

The British Airways site
uses tables to display
graphics and options

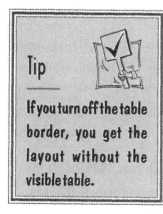

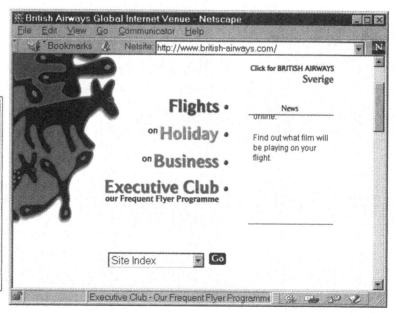

Simple table

Tables consist of cells, arranged in rows. Cells will normally fall into columns, but their widths can be set individually if required.

The first example of a table will contain two rows, two columns and no headings. A number of tags are required to define a table, commencing with the **<TABLE>** tag. Our first table is plain with no border or lines inside it, later ones will have borders and headings.

As several tags are required to create a table, it is recommended that they are indented. Remember, it is the tags that control the appearance of the page when it is viewed; indenting just makes the source code easier for you to read.

<TABLE>

You start a table with the tag **<TABLE>** and end with **</TABLE>**. Within these tags, other tags are required to define the headings, rows and the individual cells in the table.

<TR> Table row

The start of each row in the table is defined by the **<TR>** tag and the end by the **</TR>** tag.

<TD> Table data

The data for each cell in the table, is enclosed within the tags <TD> and closed with the </TD> tag. A cell ican contain text or a graphic, or be left empty.

Text can be positioned using the **ALIGN=** clause and formatted using any of the options such as <B> to bold or <BR> for a new line.

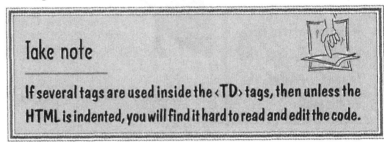

Take note

If several tags are used inside the <TD> tags, then unless the HTML is indented, you will find it hard to read and edit the code.

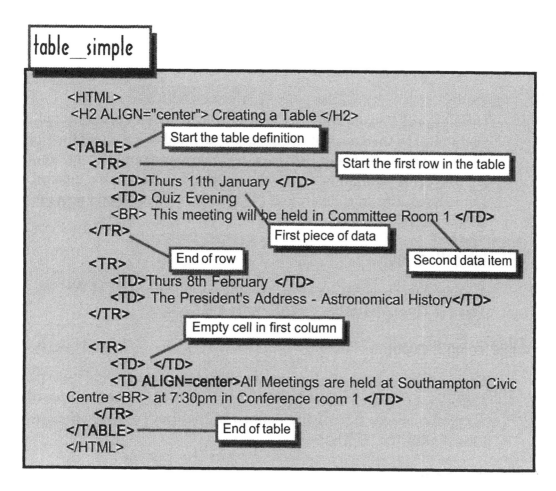

table_simple

```html
<HTML>
<H2 ALIGN="center"> Creating a Table </H2>

<TABLE>          ← Start the table definition
    <TR>         ← Start the first row in the table
        <TD>Thurs 11th January </TD>
        <TD> Quiz Evening
        <BR> This meeting will be held in Committee Room 1 </TD>
    </TR>        ← End of row
                 First piece of data / Second data item

    <TR>
        <TD>Thurs 8th February </TD>
        <TD> The President's Address - Astronomical History</TD>
    </TR>
                 ← Empty cell in first column
    <TR>
        <TD> </TD>
        <TD ALIGN=center>All Meetings are held at Southampton Civic
Centre <BR> at 7:30pm in Conference room 1 </TD>
    </TR>
</TABLE>         ← End of table
</HTML>
```

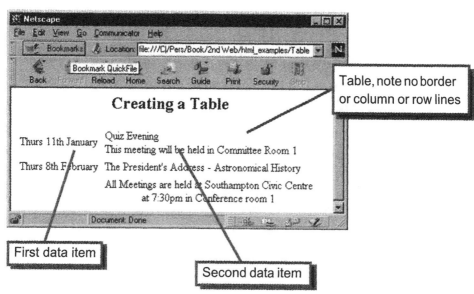

First data item

Second data item

Table, note no border or column or row lines

Borders and headings

Border=

This optional clause within the <TABLE> tag places a border around the table. The thickness of the border is defined using a number. In our example, the value of 10 makes the table stand out like a button. A little experimentation may be required to obtain the desired appearance. The spacing around the borders is controlled using the clause **CELLSPACING=**.

<CAPTION> Table Heading

A table can be given its own heading using the **<CAPTION>** tag. This is closed with the **</CAPTION>** tag.

<TH> Table column heading

Each column within a table can be allocated its own heading. The formatting options we met previously, such as **ALIGN=** can be used. A column heading is usually defined in the first row and must be closed with the **</TH>** tag.

Other format options

The space between the cell and the table can be controlled with the **CELLSPACING=** clause within the **<TABLE>** tag and the space between the sides of the cell using the **CELLPADDING=** clause.

Text can be made to span multiple columns by using the clause **COLSPAN=** inside the **<TD>** tag or multiple rows using **ROWSPAN=**.

The width of a column can be controlled using the **WIDTH=** clause inside the **<TH>** or **<TD>** tag. The width can be specified using an absolute value or as a percentage relative to the size of the table. For example, to create a column that is a quarter of the width of the table enter **<TD WIDTH=25%>**. Anyone including graphics in a table will want to use the **WIDTH=** clause to control the column size.

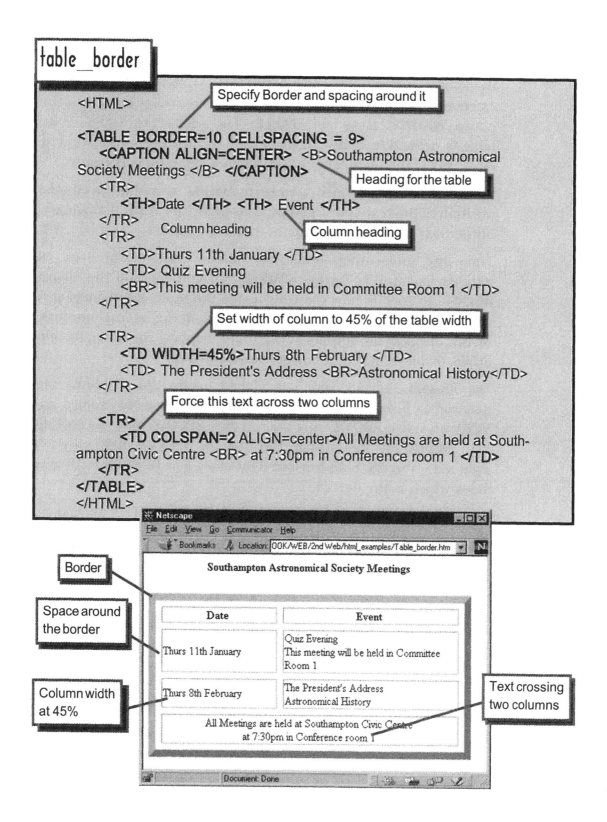

table_border

<HTML>

Specify Border and spacing around it

<TABLE BORDER=10 CELLSPACING = 9>
    <CAPTION ALIGN=CENTER> <B>Southampton Astronomical
Society Meetings </B> </CAPTION>

Heading for the table

    <TR>
        <TH>Date </TH> <TH> Event </TH>
    </TR>
    <TR>   Column heading

Column heading

        <TD>Thurs 11th January </TD>
        <TD> Quiz Evening

This meeting will be held in Committee Room 1 </TD>
    </TR>

Set width of column to 45% of the table width

    <TR>
        <TD WIDTH=45%>Thurs 8th February </TD>
        <TD> The President's Address
Astronomical History</TD>
    </TR>

Force this text across two columns

    <TR>
        <TD COLSPAN=2 ALIGN=center>All Meetings are held at South-
ampton Civic Centre <BR> at 7:30pm in Conference room 1 </TD>
    </TR>
</TABLE>
</HTML>

Border

Space around the border

Column width at 45%

Text crossing two columns

67

More table formatting

By default, the browser will set the table width to fit the screen. Alternatively, the width of the table can be controlled by adding the clause **WIDTH=** inside the **<TABLE>** tag, where the width of the table is defined in either pixels or as a percentage of the window size. This is the technique to use, when a small table is needed.

When text is being defined, the clause **ALIGN=** is used to specify the position of the text and **VALIGN=,** is used for the vertical alignment of the text, with values of top, bottom, or centre.

There are some other formatting options available for users of Internet Explorer 4. To the **<TABLE>** tag you can add the clause **RULES=,** to specify how the cells inside the table are displayed. A value of **ALL**, which is the default, displays all the internal borders, **NONE**, displays no borders, **COLS** only displays the columns and **ROWS** displays only the border between rows.

The **FRAME=** clause, which is placed inside the **<TABLE>** tag determines how the table frame is displayed. Possible values are **VOID**, no sides, **ABOVE**, only the top line, **BELOW**, only the bottom line, **HSIDES**, top and bottom, **LHS** only the left side, **RHS**, only the right side, **VSIDES**, both left and right sides and **BORDER** is all four sides which is the default.

An important point to remember when using any HTML extensions that are specific to a browser, is that if your reader isn't using that browser, then your page will not be displayed exactly as it was designed.

Tip

Internet Explorer can be downloaded from Microsoft's web site at http://www.microsoft.com

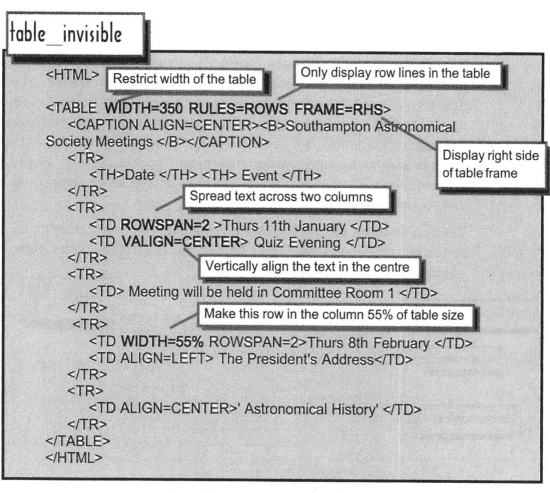

table_invisible

```
<HTML>                 [Restrict width of the table]          [Only display row lines in the table]

<TABLE WIDTH=350 RULES=ROWS FRAME=RHS>
    <CAPTION ALIGN=CENTER><B>Southampton Astronomical
Society Meetings </B></CAPTION>
    <TR>                                                     [Display right side
        <TH>Date </TH> <TH> Event </TH>                      of table frame]
    </TR>          [Spread text across two columns]
    <TR>
        <TD ROWSPAN=2 >Thurs 11th January </TD>
        <TD VALIGN=CENTER> Quiz Evening </TD>
    </TR>          [Vertically align the text in the centre]
    <TR>
        <TD> Meeting will be held in Committee Room 1 </TD>
    </TR>          [Make this row in the column 55% of table size]
    <TR>
        <TD WIDTH=55% ROWSPAN=2>Thurs 8th February </TD>
        <TD ALIGN=LEFT> The President's Address</TD>
    </TR>
    <TR>
        <TD ALIGN=CENTER>' Astronomical History' </TD>
    </TR>
</TABLE>
</HTML>
```

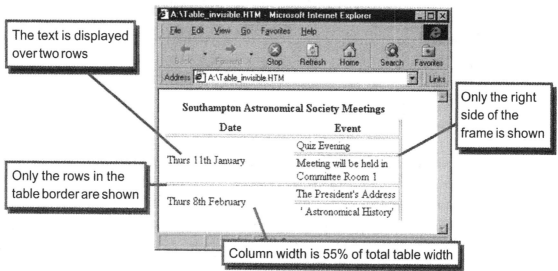

The text is displayed over two rows

Only the right side of the frame is shown

Only the rows in the table border are shown

Column width is 55% of total table width

A:\Table_invisible.HTM - Microsoft Internet Explorer

File Edit View Go Favorites Help

Address A:\Table_invisible.HTM

Southampton Astronomical Society Meetings

Date	Event
Thurs 11th January	Quiz Evening
	Meeting will be held in Committee Room 1
Thurs 8th February	The President's Address
	' Astronomical History'

Tables in Netscape Composer

To construct a table requires a number of tags, therefore this is a good time to consider using a tool like Netscape Composer. The first step is to click on the Table icon and the display shown below appears. Here you define the characteristics of the table such as number of columns and rows, whether you want a border, the background colour and various alignment options. Simply answer these questions, click on the *OK* button and the table appears as shown opposite.

Remember all those tags we had to remember and how tricky it was to construct a line in the table? Using this tool, that is now a thing of the past.

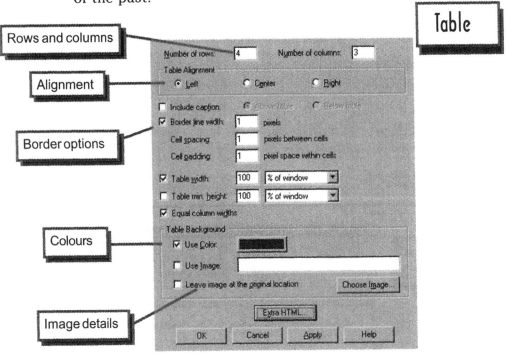

When our table appears, to enter something into a cell simple click on it and if it's, text start typing. Frequently tables without borders hold graphics and they can also be specified here.

To include a graphic in the table, position yourself in the cell where the graphic is to be placed and click on the **image** icon and a window is provided which requests the name of the graphic file. Simply fill in the details about the image and it will appear.

Cells in the table could also include a link to another Web site or page which is created by clicking on the **link** icon.

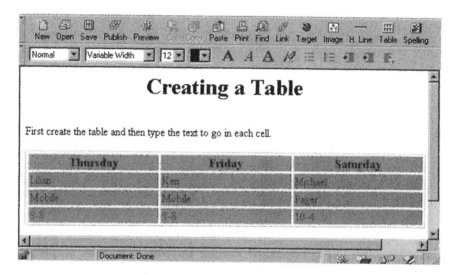

What is nice about this approach, is that really complex HTML is being written behind the scenes, but you can see how the table will appear while you are constructing it. In addition, all the table options are visible when completing the dialog box, thereby reminding the designer of what can be done using a table.

Another approach to consider is create just the table using this or another editor. Once you are happy with the look of it, save the HTML and then insert this code into your master document.

Tables in FrontPage Express

The method used to create a table in Front Page Express is very similar to the approach used by Netscape Composer.

Click on the table icon that appears in the main window, then to specify how big the table is to be, click on the right-most box that represents the size that you want, or point to the top left box and drag to set the size – if you want more than 5 columns or 4 rows, just keep dragging off the grid!

Alternatively, open the *Table* menu and select *Insert Table*. The dialog box shown opposite is displayed where you answer a few simple questions such as number of rows and columns and whether borders are needed. Clicking on the *OK* button, the table is instantly displayed on your Web page. Once the table is visible, to include text in the table, click on the desired cell and start typing.

The characteristics of the table or cell can be modified at any time by using the right mouse button. This will display a another dialog box where you can specify the size of the borders and colours.

If table headings are required, they should be entered as per any text in the table and don't forget that at any time the HTML source for the table can be displayed.

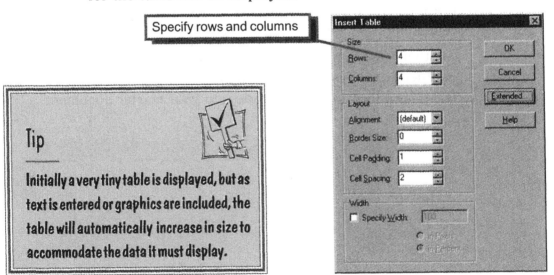

Specify rows and columns

Tip

Initially a very tiny table is displayed, but as text is entered or graphics are included, the table will automatically increase in size to accommodate the data it must display.

Style sheets

Before the introduction of style sheets, it wasn't easy to define all the characteristics of a Web page when the default display attributes were unsuitable. With the introduction of the <STYLE> tag, it is now possible to define precisely how information is to be displayed. It is part of the HTML 4.0 specification, therefore it may not be supported by your browser if you have an older version.

A style sheet can be included in your document, or it may be referenced from an Internet site. There are many options that can be included in a style sheet and a good external reference can be found on the Web at http://www.w3j.com/5/s2.lie.html

Ideally, the style sheet should be defined at the start of the document, but this is not mandatory. It must be placed before you want to use any of the defined styles. It begins with the <STYLE> tag and closes with the </STYLE> tag. Within these, you describe the options for each of the formatting tags. Therefore to specify how a level 1 heading is to appear, you write H1 then specify the options within { } brackets. Each option is separated with a semicolon and the format for each option is specified after the colon. For example, heading 1 must appear with a font size of 22pt, using the Courier font and in black, is defined in the style sheet as

H1 { font: 22pt Courier; color:black }

All of the HTML tags may be controlled in this fashion, which means that we can use different fonts and text colours for each level and paragraph. Other items that can be controlled include the background colour and image and the bullet to be used on lists. For the Web page itself, an extensive number of options are available to control margin size, space around the borders and sizing and for lists. It doesn't matter in which order the options are written.

Only one style sheet can be assigned to an HTML document, but each document can use its own style sheet. Once style sheets are in use, rather than repeat all of these tags in every document, the style sheet is stored with your Web documents and referenced directly from the HTML document instead. (See page XX for more on this.)

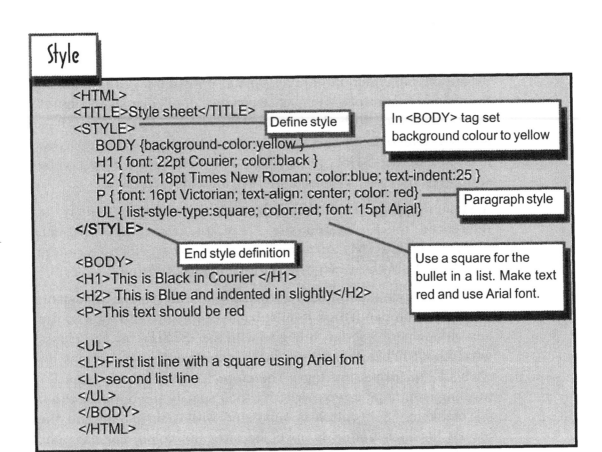

Style

```
<HTML>
<TITLE>Style sheet</TITLE>
<STYLE>
    BODY {background-color:yellow}
    H1 { font: 22pt Courier; color:black }
    H2 { font: 18pt Times New Roman; color:blue; text-indent:25 }
    P { font: 16pt Victorian; text-align: center; color: red}
    UL { list-style-type:square; color:red; font: 15pt Arial}
</STYLE>

<BODY>
<H1>This is Black in Courier </H1>
<H2> This is Blue and indented in slightly</H2>
<P>This text should be red

<UL>
<LI>First list line with a square using Ariel font
<LI>second list line
</UL>
</BODY>
</HTML>
```

Define style

In <BODY> tag set background colour to yellow

Paragraph style

End style definition

Use a square for the bullet in a list. Make text red and use Arial font.

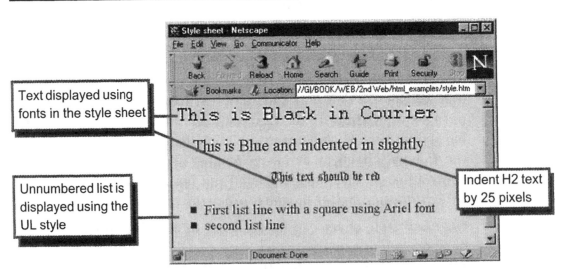

Text displayed using fonts in the style sheet

Unnumbered list is displayed using the UL style

Indent H2 text by 25 pixels

74

Using a style sheet will enable you to format a Web page using options that are not available in regular HTML. Since it is also easier to customise the tags, it is possible to create some rather nice effects using the different options. Shown here are some more style sheet options.

To specify the background image and how it should repeat use

BODY { background-image: url(at_work.gif); background-repeat: repeat }

Several repeat options are available: *repeat*; *repeat-x* only repeat horizontally; *repeat-y* only repeat vertically; and *norepeat* to only display the image once.

Here are some more text formatting options. Define a margin that starts 1 inch from the left, create a thick border around the text, set the text colour to green and set the style of the text so that the first letter is shown in capitals.

P {margin: 1in; border-width:thick; color:green; text-transform:capitalize}

Below we changed the style of the font to italic, set the thickness of the font to 100, but the value could be anything up to 900 and request that the text is indented by 25% of the browser window size.

P {font-style:italic; font-weight:100; text-indent:25%}

The margins can be controlled using the following clauses where the values are specified either as a percentage or as an actual measurement, such as 0.5 inches.

P {margin-left: 1in; margin-right: 2in; margin-top:25%;
   margin-bottom:10%}

Tip

If you want several pages to use the same styles, you can create a default style sheet and link this from the pages. See page 111.

Summary

In this chapter we have see more techniques that can be used in our Web document for including text. Some of them such as lists and tables, have been introduced for text, but can be used for other things. Style sheets are easy to include in our documents and provide a means to create some nice effects on our Web page.

Now you should be ready to try writing some more HTML to achieve the following:

❑ change the fonts and colours;

❑ display information in list;

❑ use a table to display some text;

❑ create several Web documents and then jump from one document to the next;

❑ identify external Web sites that could be referenced from your Web site;

❑ use some style sheets on your documents so that they look different from typical Web pages that you have seen.

4 Graphics

Why use graphics 78

Including graphics 80

Text and spaces around a graphic . . 82

Alternative text 84

Transparent images 85

Fast graphic display 86

Using your photos 87

Graphics in tables 88

Graphics using HTML editors 91

Backgrounds 93

Summary 96

Why use graphics

Web sites that comprise of only text, may be informative, but are considered 'boring'. Commercial sites are typically, bright and lively using **graphics** to promote their products or services. There are many ways pictures can be used on a Web page for instance:

- to show a scene or provide information;
- an icon;
- a background;
- for graphs;
- to display a logo;
- to display a product;
- banner;
- line;
- navigation map.

Graphics are used extensively on Web sites because many designers feel that a picture can say a thousand words. Suppose you are car manufacturer, a potential buyer is interested in not only the technical specification of the car and accessories, but also its appearance. By providing pictures of the car at different angles, they can take a virtual tour of the vehicle from the comfort of their chair.

On a personal Web site, if your family is scattered around the globe. Rather than send them the latest pictures of the family, you could keep them on your Web site and advise them everytime it is updated.

An important point to consider when designing your Web page, is the size of each of the graphic files. If your audience is likely to be people at home then bear in mind the sometimes slow speed of the Internet, and the high probability that they are not using the latest and fastest modems, they could wait a long time displaying the images. Therefore, if this is a commercial site, you could easily lose business.

Graphic file formats

There are a number of different file formats in which graphics can be stored such as PCX, TIFF or BMP. Web browsers like their graphics stored in GIF or JPEG formats, neither of which can be produced by Windows Paintbrush. However, this is not a problem as there are shareware tools which will convert files from PCX or BMP formats to GIF or JPEG format. These include, Wingif and Paint Shop Pro.

GIF

GIF files are extremely popular on Web sites. Although they are limited to 256 colours, they still display good images. The compression on GIF files is not the best, therefore they won't be stored using the fewest bytes. However, they are ideal on Web pages for simple, low-resolution tasks, such as icons, logos and low resolution pictures.

JPEG

The JPEG format stores an image using millions of colour and it compresses the image much better than the GIF format. Therefore your images occupy less storage space, are smaller to transfer, but take a little longer to display because of the more complex compression algorithms in use. JPEG images are ideal for displaying high quality colour images, especially photographic quality or any image that needs more than 256 colours.

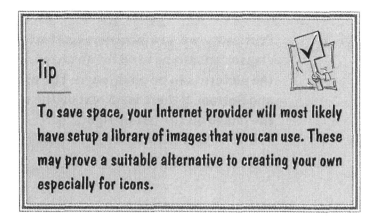

Tip

To save space, your Internet provider will most likely have setup a library of images that you can use. These may prove a suitable alternative to creating your own especially for icons.

Including graphics

A graphic can be included anywhere on a Web page, but you cannot specify exactly where it is to be located, unless you use a table which provides a little more control. There are a number of extra qualifiers which can be added to the basic image tag, which will affect how the text is positioned around the graphic, but not the position of the graphic itself.

<IMG> Image

The **<IMG>** tag is used to place a graphic on a Web page . To specify the name of the graphic, you must add the parameter **SRC=**

SRC= Source file

Specify the name of the file containing the picture. Normally one only has to give the file name, but should it be located in another directory, then you must add the full path name into the **SRC=** clause.

When the HTML document is loaded onto the Internet, you will also have to copy all the graphic files as well. Your HTML document may only occupy 2–5 kilobytes, but each graphic file could be 20Kb or more. Therefore you may only have to include several image files before you exceed a quota set by your service provider. However, many service providers are generous and offer 5, even 25 megabytes of storage which should allow many graphics files to be displayed.

ALIGN=

Previously we saw how to align text using the **ALIGN=** clause. This clause can also be used for an image. It specifies how the text around the picture is to be positioned. The options available are **Top**, **Middle** and **Bottom**. If there is no text on the line, then you can use it to place the image on the left or right.

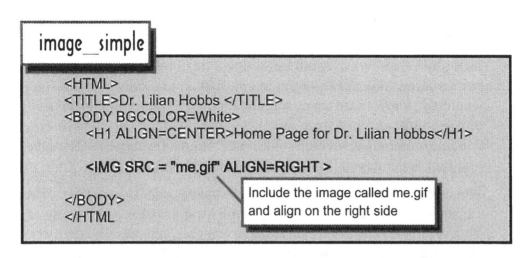

```
<HTML>
<TITLE>Dr. Lilian Hobbs </TITLE>
<BODY BGCOLOR=White>
    <H1 ALIGN=CENTER>Home Page for Dr. Lilian Hobbs</H1>

    <IMG SRC = "me.gif" ALIGN=RIGHT >

</BODY>
</HTML
```

Include the image called me.gif and align on the right side

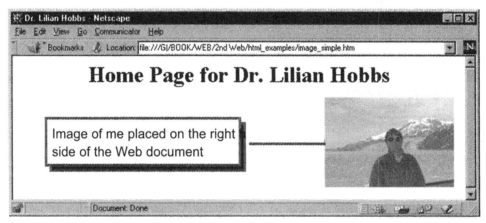

Home Page for Dr. Lilian Hobbs

Image of me placed on the right side of the Web document

Missing Graphic

When a graphic cannot be found, browsers will display a question mark like this one

Tip

You must specify the name of the graphic file, exactly as it appears in the file system, using upper and lowercase letters as shown in the file name. If you do not, the link may not work when the files are uploaded to the Web server.

Text and spaces around a graphic

A graphic on its own may not be sufficient to convey the full message. For instance, look at the example opposite. If you only saw the star, would you know that this meant clicking here gives you information on the Southampton Astronomical Society? Probably not. Therefore, it is quite common to include some text around a graphic or alternative text that is displayed if the graphic is not displayed.

When graphics are displayed, no blank space is put around them. This can have the effect of making the graphics appear too close together,. To overcome this problem, two parameters can be added to the <IMG> tag to specify how much space is to be left around the graphic. The number specified is in terms of pixels and a number in the range 5 to 30 is usually suitable.

HSPACE=

Reserves horizontal space on the left and right of the graphic.

VSPACE=

Reserves vertical space at the top and bottom of the graphic.

Width= Height=

Used together, height and width specify the size of the image. The browser will automatically adjust the image to fit in the size specified. The values can be given in pixels, or as a percentage of the width or height of the browser window.

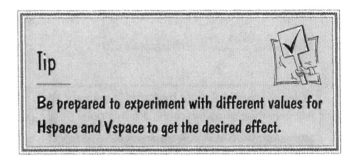

Tip

Be prepared to experiment with different values for Hspace and Vspace to get the desired effect.

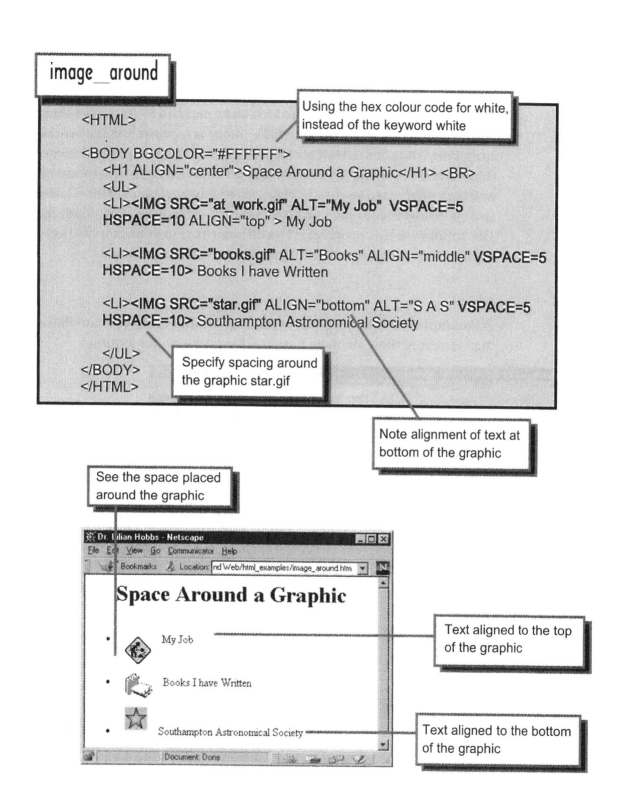

image_around

Using the hex colour code for white, instead of the keyword white

```
<HTML>

<BODY BGCOLOR="#FFFFFF">
    <H1 ALIGN="center">Space Around a Graphic</H1> <BR>
    <UL>
    <LI><IMG SRC="at_work.gif" ALT="My Job"  VSPACE=5
    HSPACE=10 ALIGN="top" > My Job

    <LI><IMG SRC="books.gif" ALT="Books" ALIGN="middle" VSPACE=5
    HSPACE=10> Books I have Written

    <LI><IMG SRC="star.gif" ALIGN="bottom" ALT="S A S" VSPACE=5
    HSPACE=10> Southampton Astronomical Society

    </UL>
</BODY>
</HTML>
```

Specify spacing around the graphic star.gif

Note alignment of text at bottom of the graphic

See the space placed around the graphic

Text aligned to the top of the graphic

Text aligned to the bottom of the graphic

Alternative text

How many times have you visited a Web site and had to stare at a blank screen while you are waiting for the image to appear? At the worst sites, the visitor has to wait for all the graphics to be displayed before they can do anything. If your visitors are patient, they will not mind waiting, otherwise they are likely to give heavy-graphics sites a miss and go elsewhere. Some surfers even turn off images downloading. The solution to this problem is to add some text to your graphic tags, so that text is displayed if the graphic has not been loaded.

Alt=

Tthe simplest way to do this is by adding the **ALT=** clause to the **<IMG>** tag. Its text is then displayed as an alternative to the graphic.

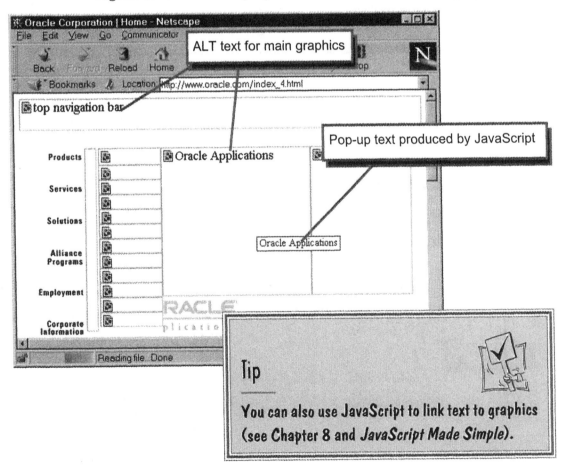

Transparent images

Using transparent GIF files on your Web site can add some very nice effects. When an image is saved as transparent, using a tool such as Paint Shop Pro, one selected colour will not be displayed. In Paint Shop Pro, you can specify that the transparent colour be automatically set to the background colour on the Web page. In the example below, the image is saved with a background colour of grey set to transparent. When it is displayed the background colour is white – the screen background colour. An ideal use for transparent images is a logo.

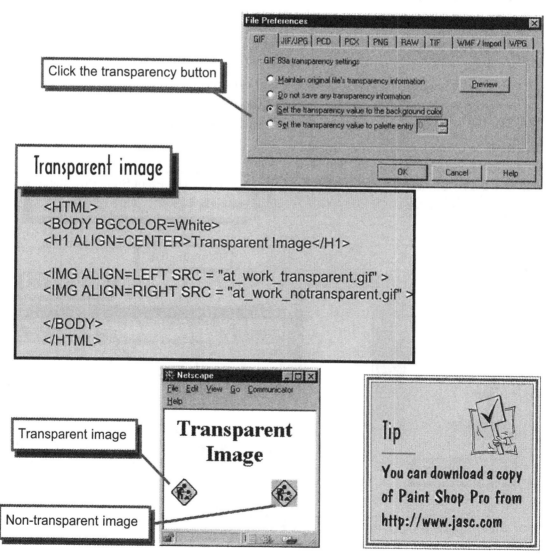

Click the transparency button

Transparent image

```
<HTML>
<BODY BGCOLOR=White>
<H1 ALIGN=CENTER>Transparent Image</H1>

<IMG ALIGN=LEFT SRC = "at_work_transparent.gif" >
<IMG ALIGN=RIGHT SRC = "at_work_notransparent.gif" >

</BODY>
</HTML>
```

Transparent image

Non-transparent image

Tip

You can download a copy of Paint Shop Pro from http://www.jasc.com

Fast graphic display

A Web page with a lot of graphics can take a long time to load. If the user has to wait for the entire image to be displayed before they can findout what it is, this can be very frustrating, especially if they have a slow Internet connection or the Internet is running slowly.

The way to overcome this problem is to use GIF files which are saved as **89a-Interlaced type**. An interlaced GIF file appears to the reader as if it is coming into focus slowly. It first appears hazy and then gradually the image appears. This techniqueis particularly useful with large images that may take some time to load.

Creating interlaced GIFs

Creating interlaced GIFs is not difficult as long as you have the right tool, and Paint Shop Pro is an ideal tool for the job. All you have to do is select the right type (GIF) and sub-type (Version 89a - interlaced) when you save the file.

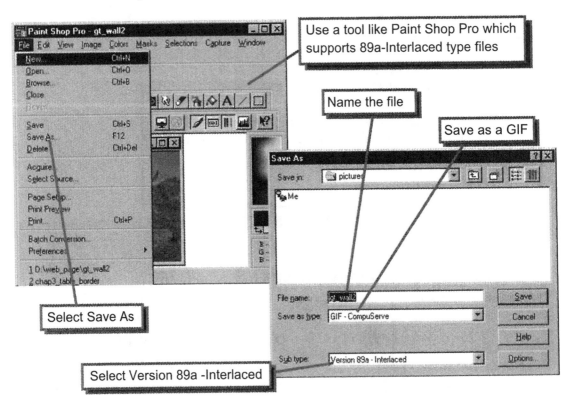

Use a tool like Paint Shop Pro which supports 89a-Interlaced type files

Name the file

Save as a GIF

Select Save As

Select Version 89a -Interlaced

Using your photos

One of the attractions of a Web page is the ability to share personal information with farflung family, or interests with fellow enthusiasts. Would you like to show those family snaps to distant relatives? Or in the commercial world, would you like to display your products. Here are three different ways to put photographs on your Web site.

Kodak Photo CD

Kodak Photo CD allows you to take a picture with an ordinary camera and from the negative, have the picture transferred onto a computer CD. Many photographic shops offer this service, which typically takes about a week. Programs like Paint Shop Pro can read the CD and display the picture. One hundred images will fit on a CD, and when reduced in size and converted to JPEG or GIF format they are suitable for inclusion on a Web page.

Digital cameras

Digital cameras are a recent innovation and are rapidly growing in popularity. They are very like ordinary cameras to use, but don't have any film and you can see the results immediately, so if you don't like the picture you can throw it away. A digital camera can only store a limited number of pictures and then they must be transferred to a computer. This is achieved by connecting the camera to the computer by a cable and using its companion transfer software. You can then view the pictures again and decide whether to discard or keep them.

Scanners

Until recently flat-bed scanners, where you could lay a photograph down and have it scanned. were primarily found in commercial organisations. Fortunately, they are now available to the home user for well under one hundred pounds.

Using a scanner you can take any photograph, or picture from your company's catalogue, capture it using the software provided and then save it as a GIF image which is then displayed on your Web site.

Graphics in tables

Many Web designers prefer to place their graphics inside a table, because the table provides a means of placing multiple graphics on a line with spacing and text.

A graphic is inserted in a table by placing the <IMG> tag with all the graphic options between the table tags <TD> and </TD>. The only problem with using this approach is that the HTML required to implement this, is a bit difficult to read.

When using a table for the graphics, you can disable the border so that the reader doesn't realise that a table is being used. Also, take advantage of clauses such as ROWSPAN= and COLSPAN= to force the image across multiple columns or rows.

Many sites use tables and a good example of graphics on a Web page inside a table is the one below from the Yellow Pages site.

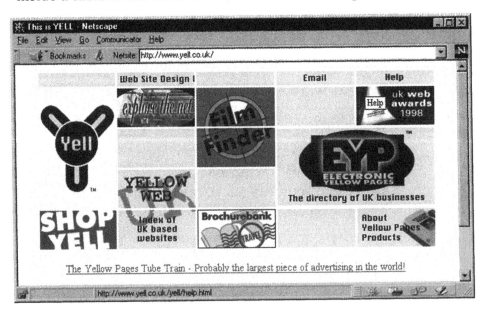

A table doesn't have to include many images. At the NASA Eclipse Web site, a single table is used to display the banner at the top of the page (see opposite). The second example, from the Armagh Observatory Web site, uses one table to display the two images of Comet Hyakutake and a different table to store just the image for Comet Hale-Bopp.

```
<HTML>
<CENTER><TABLE BORDER=5 CELLSPACING=5>
<TR><TH>
<IMG SRC="image/bannerEclipse.gif" WIDTH=504 HEIGHT=115
      HSPACE=3 VSPACE=3 ALT="Eclipse Banner">
</TH></TR></TABLE></CENTER>
</HTML>
```

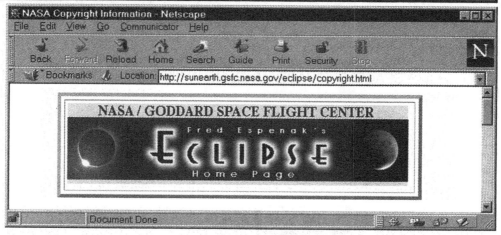

Click on any of these thumbnail images to display the large image

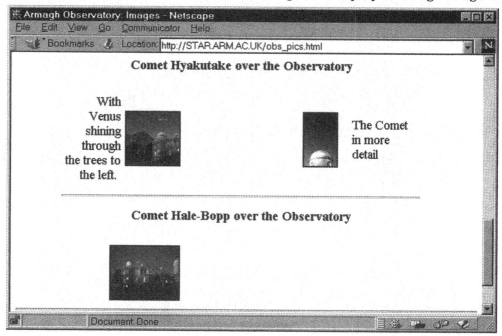

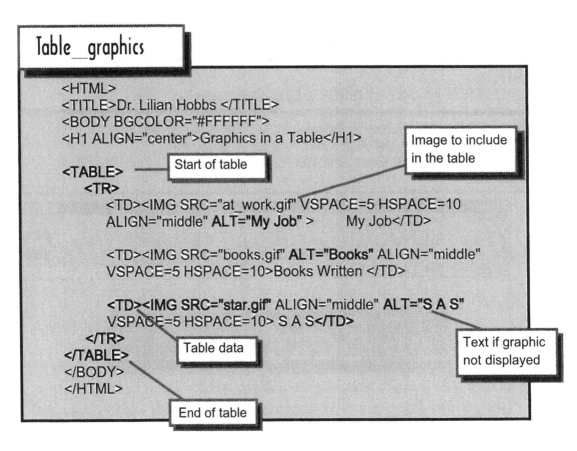

```
<HTML>
<TITLE>Dr. Lilian Hobbs </TITLE>
<BODY BGCOLOR="#FFFFFF">
<H1 ALIGN="center">Graphics in a Table</H1>

<TABLE>
   <TR>
      <TD><IMG SRC="at_work.gif" VSPACE=5 HSPACE=10
      ALIGN="middle" ALT="My Job" >        My Job</TD>

      <TD><IMG SRC="books.gif" ALT="Books" ALIGN="middle"
      VSPACE=5 HSPACE=10>Books Written </TD>

      <TD><IMG SRC="star.gif" ALIGN="middle" ALT="S A S"
      VSPACE=5 HSPACE=10> S A S</TD>
   </TR>
</TABLE>
</BODY>
</HTML>
```

Image to include in the table

Start of table

Table data

Text if graphic not displayed

End of table

Invisible table

Graphics in three columns in the table

90

Graphics using HTML editors

Netscape Composer

In Netscape Composer a graphic is included by clicking on the graphic icon. This opens the dialog box shown below, and here you specify the name of the file to be displayed. The added benefit of using this approach is that you can also specify how the text is to be wrapped around the image, the alignment and spacing of the image plus other options.

The same technique is used whenever a graphic is included on the Web page, such as inserting it into a table. This is also the place where you would specify that the graphic is to be used as a background image (see page 93).

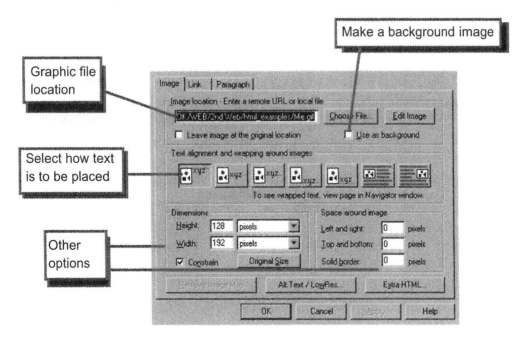

Make a background image

Graphic file location

Select how text is to be placed

Other options

FrontPage Express

To include a graphic using FrontPage Express, click on the image icon to specify the file. The options for placing the graphic on the page are not included on this form. Instead, use the right mouse button and click while over the image to display the *Image Properties* page. Then click on the *Appearance* tab to specify how the image is to be placed.

The image is aligned on the page by clicking on the alignment options that are used for text paragraphs. As for how the text wraps around the image, you may not be able to create the desired effect with this cutdown version of the tool. However, that shouldn't dissuade you from using it, because you can always modify the generated HTML.

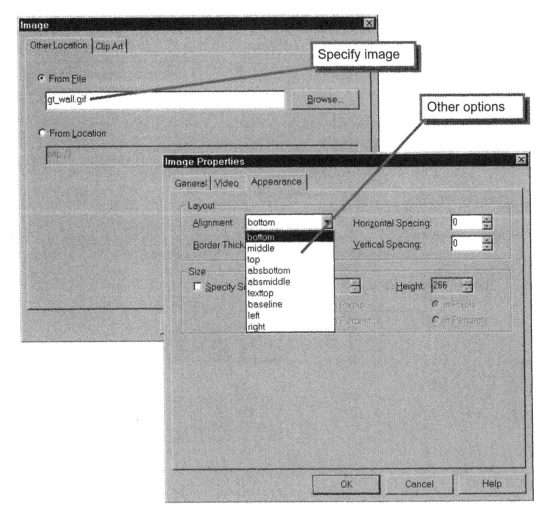

Backgrounds

There is another way to liven up your Web page and that is to include a background image. These are usually small images which are repeated across and down the page. There are some wonderful ones around on the Internet or you can create your own. It's worth checking if your service provider has a library of background images that you can use. If not, then any JPEG or GIF image can be included, although not all are suitable. For example, the background shown opposite for this Babylon 5 Web site is perfect. It sets the scene nicely for the topic to be discussed.

<BODY BACKGROUND = >

To use a background image, add the clause **BACKGROUND=** to the <BODY> tag at the top of the HTML document. Within the quotes, specify the name of the graphic file to be used as the background.

Netscape provide some backgrounds at:

http://www.netscape.com/assist/net_sites/bg/backgrounds.html

which you could reference directly from your Web site. However, this isn't recommended as it will make your Web site slower to display. Instead download the image to your site and save it as a separate file.

The clever design of the Babylon 5 background hides the fact that this is a repeated image. Sometimes you want the repeat to show up, to create a deliberate pattern, as in this example from the Southampton Astronomical Society.

See the next page for the source code for this display

Background image

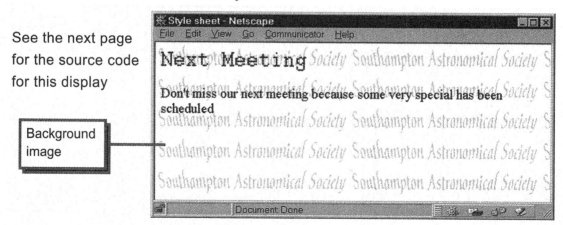

Babylon 5
has a great
background!

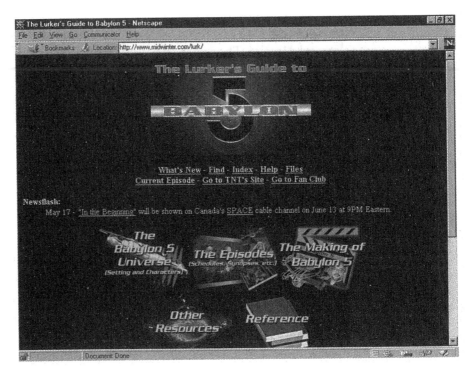

Background using a Style Sheet

On page 75, we met the idea of setting up a background image in a
style sheet. Here's an example of this in use.

back__sas

```
<HTML>
<TITLE>Style sheet</TITLE>                    set background options
<STYLE>
    BODY { background-image: url(SAS.gif) ; background-repeat: repeat }
    H1 { font: 22pt Courier; color:black }
    P { font: 16pt Victorian; text-align: center; color: red ;}
</STYLE>
<BODY>
 <H1>Next Meeting</H1>
 Don't miss our next meeting because some very special has been sched-
uled
 </BODY>
 </HTML>
```

Creating a Background

A background image can be created using any image tool. For example, this background image for the Southampton Astronmical Society was created using CorelDraw, simply by writing the text, then stretching the text using the tools provided and then changing the colour to a very light shade of gray so that it does not obscure the text or graphics that will be on the page.

When creating a background, it is very important to select colours or images that will blend into the background. For example, if these words were in black, then any black text on the page would be very hard to see.

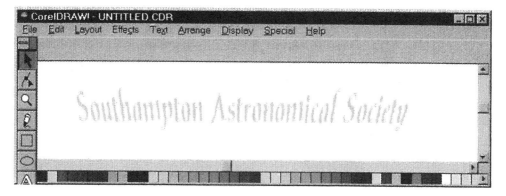

Another factor to consider is the size of the image, the smaller the image, the more times it will repeat on the page.

Finally the image should be saved as a GIF file and then moved into the folder with all the other HTML documents.

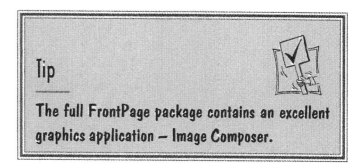

Tip

The full FrontPage package contains an excellent graphics application – Image Composer.

Summary

We have now seen how to include graphics on our Web page which is not difficult, but we do need to consider the type of image and its size and whether to use an interlaced file which will come into focus gradually.

Backgrounds can be easily added to our image and we can create our own so that they are suitable for the topic under discussion.

Useful techniques to practise would be:

❑ including a graphic, individually and in lists and experiment with the different spacing options and use of alternative text;

❑ create some transparent images and interlaced gif images;

❑ try different types of backgrounds and see how some backgrounds are not suitable because it prevents the text and other graphics being readily visible.

5 Links

Jumping 98

Multiple pages 100

Linking to other pages 102

Jumping with graphics 104

Image maps 106

Using image maps 107

Mapedit 109

Default style sheets 111

Summary 112

Jumping

A Web page may contain information on a number of topics which is often presented in the form of a list. HTML provides a mechanism, a **hypertext link**, which allows the reader to jump to a certain point in a page – or to any other page, in the same set or elsewhere.

Any document that is long or broken into sections should contain hypertext links, which can be located in headings, text, bulleted lists or in image maps.

To jump from one place to another in an HTML document requires two tags:

1 <A HREF=>

1 <A NAME=>

<A HREF= "# "> Jump From

This tag is positioned at the point you wish to jump *from*. It is given the name (with a preceding #) of the point you wish to jump *to*, and can be enclosed in "quotes" if desired, e.g. **<A HREF = "#B5">**. Immediately following the tag, specify some text to explain where you will be jumping too. This text is highlighted by the browser so choose something meaningful. Close with the </A> tag.

<A NAME=" "> Jump To

This tag is placed in the document at the point which you want to jump to. The name must match the name specified at the jump point, but without the preceding #. The tag is closed using the </A> tag.

In the example opposite, we give the jump point the label B5 and then place the text Babylon 5 after it. Later in the document at the point where the text on Babylon 5 starts, we place the label B5 inside the <A> tag.

The technique described here can only be used to jump to points within the same HTML document, a very slightly different approach is required to jump to another HTML document.

Jumping

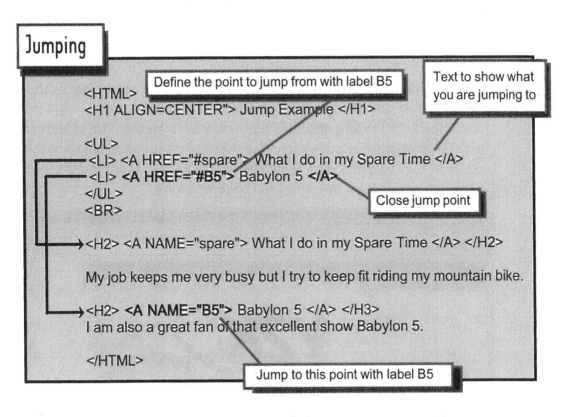

Define the point to jump from with label B5

Text to show what you are jumping to

```
<HTML>
<H1 ALIGN=CENTER"> Jump Example </H1>

<UL>
<LI> <A HREF="#spare"> What I do in my Spare Time </A>
<LI> <A HREF="#B5"> Babylon 5 </A>
</UL>
<BR>

<H2> <A NAME="spare"> What I do in my Spare Time </A> </H2>

My job keeps me very busy but I try to keep fit riding my mountain bike.

<H2> <A NAME="B5"> Babylon 5 </A> </H3>
I am also a great fan of that excellent show Babylon 5.

</HTML>
```

Close jump point

Jump to this point with label B5

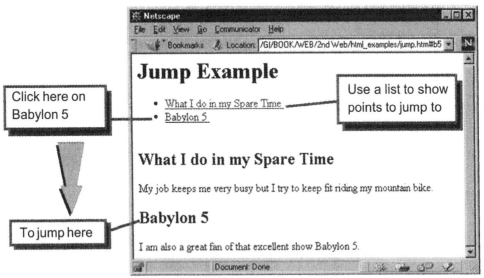

Click here on Babylon 5

Use a list to show points to jump to

To jump here

99

Multiple pages

A Web site usually comprises of multiple pages, each one a separate HTML document. With this approach, documents are smaller, and therefore easier to maintain and faster to retrieve and display. Commercial sites in particular use many Web pages. For example, from this page from the Oracle Corporation, you can move to other areas of the company such as products or events. It is not uncommon for each product to have its own page or pages.

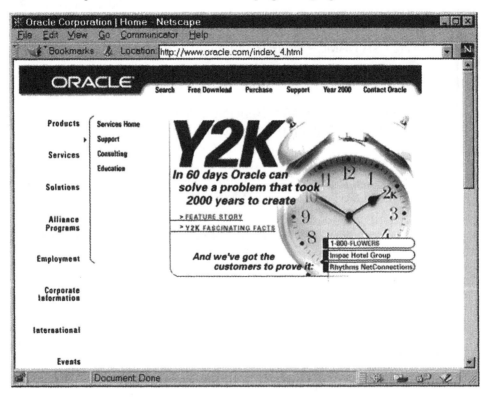

Open another Web page <A HREF=" ">

To move from one Web page to another, the tag **<A HREF=" "** > is used with the name of the target HTML page written inside the quotes. For example, to jump to a page called "self.html", the tag would be:

<A HREF= "self.html">Some text </A>

To return to your home page, add another <A HREF> tag with the name of the home page document.

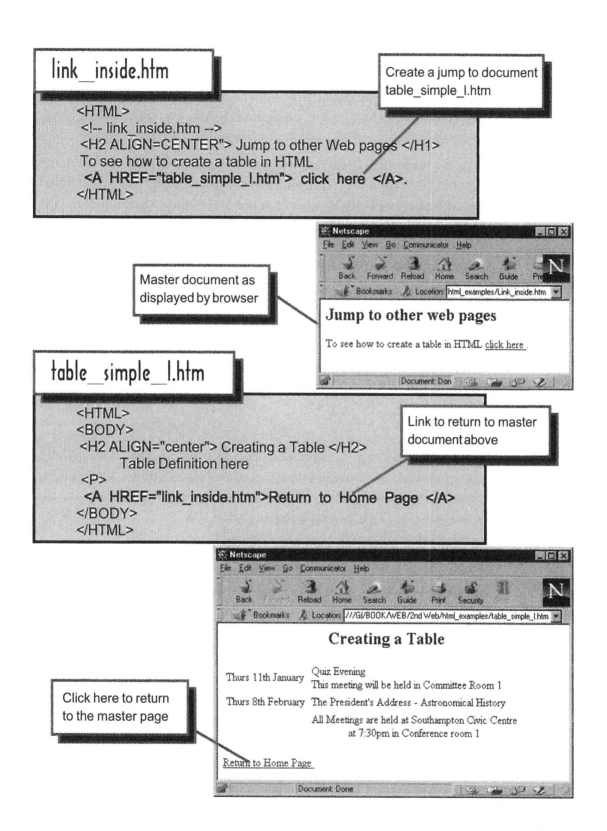

link_ inside.htm

Create a jump to document table_simple_l.htm

```
<HTML>
<!-- link_inside.htm -->
<H2 ALIGN=CENTER"> Jump to other Web pages </H1>
To see how to create a table in HTML
<A HREF="table_simple_l.htm"> click here </A>.
</HTML>
```

Master document as displayed by browser

Netscape
File Edit View Go Communicator Help
Back Forward Reload Home Search Guide Pri
Bookmarks Location html_examples/Link_inside.htm

Jump to other web pages

To see how to create a table in HTML click here .

Document Don

table_ simple_ l.htm

```
<HTML>
<BODY>
<H2 ALIGN="center"> Creating a Table </H2>
      Table Definition here
<P>
<A HREF="link_inside.htm">Return to Home Page </A>
</BODY>
</HTML>
```

Link to return to master document above

Netscape
File Edit View Go Communicator Help
Back Forward Reload Home Search Guide Print Security
Bookmarks Location ///GI/BOOK/WEB/2nd Web/html_examples/table_simple_l.htm

Creating a Table

Thurs 11th January   Quiz Evening
                      This meeting will be held in Committee Room 1

Thurs 8th February   The President's Address - Astronomical History

                      All Meetings are held at Southampton Civic Centre
                      at 7:30pm in Conference room 1

Click here to return to the master page

Return to Home Page

Document Done

Linking to other pages

One of the nice features of the Internet is the ability to jump from one page to another, using a hypertext link. By referencing other Web pages you start to exploit the potential of the Internet.

Links to Web sites external to your own are desirable for many reasons. For example, to provide more information from a specialist site, or link to a manufacturer or a special event. Although we shall only be looking at jumping from this Web page, remember that you can ask people to provide a link to be able to jump to your page. To specify a jump point, two pieces of information are needed:

1   the Internet address of the place you wish to jump to

1   some text or an icon or both to describe the jump point

A jump point is easy to see on a Web page because it will be displayed in a different colour and underlined so that it stands out from the other text.

Jump to <A HREF= " ">

The **<A HREF=>** tag is used to define the link to the external site. Simply include the Internet address of the place you wish to jump to between the quotes. Then add some text to describe where you will be jumping to. Finally close the tag with </A>.

<A HREF="http://www.oracle.com"> Oracle </A>

If any site is going to include a link to your page, then they would have to include an <A HREF=> tag with your address on their Web page.

Tip

Web sites frequently change. It's a good idea to regularly check your external jump points to see they are still valid.

Jump to another page

Create a link to the Star Trek site

```
<HTML>
<H1 ALIGN=CENTER> Link to another web site </H1>
<P>When I get time I like to watch TV, two of my favourite TV shows are
<A HREF="http://www.startrek.com/startrek.asp"> Star Trek
Voyager </A> and <A HREF="http://www.babylon5.com/ "> Babylon 5
</A>. To find out more about these shows click on the name here.
</HTML>
```

As document appears in a browser

Clicking on Star Trek Voyager displays this page

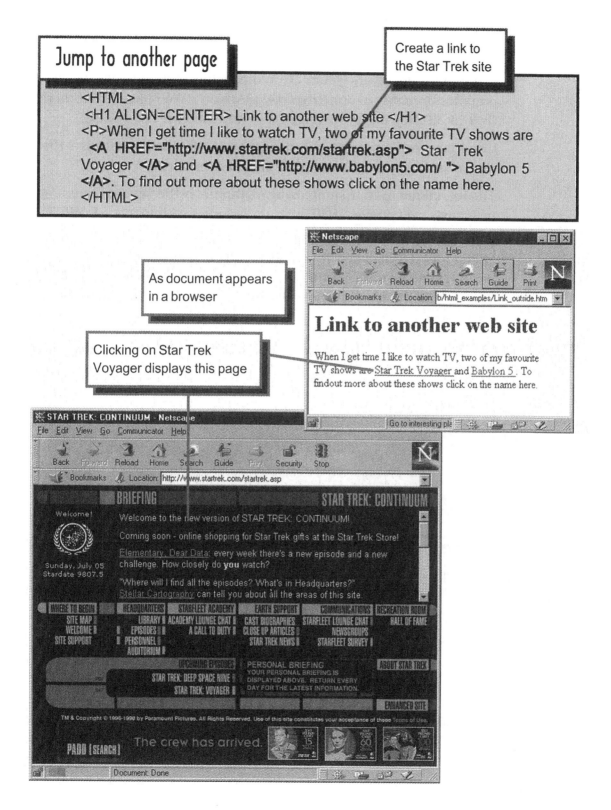

Jumping with graphics

Many Web designers seem to avoid using text and like to use graphics or icons to jump from one place on a Web page to another. Best of all they make the page look good and are fun to use.

Graphics used as jump points are easy to identify because the cursor changes to a hand when placed over them.

The technique used to jump using a graphic, is the same as jumping with text, except the **<IMG>** tag is included within the **<A HREF>** tag. The browser will automatically associate the picture with the jump point. Referring to the example below, to see Alan Bean's new print called Homeward Bound, all we have to do is click anywhere on the small image of it to learn more about that print and findout the price.

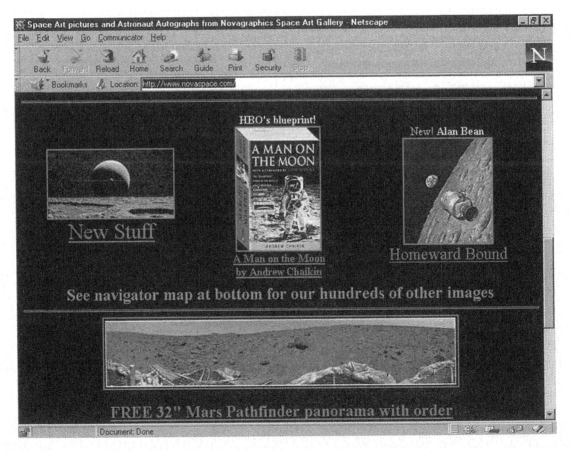

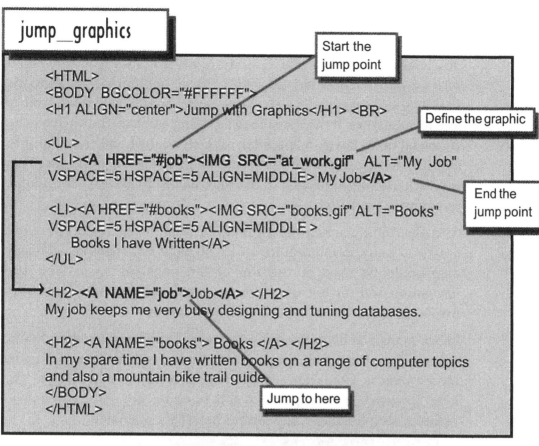

jump__graphics

```
<HTML>
<BODY BGCOLOR="#FFFFFF">
<H1 ALIGN="center">Jump with Graphics</H1> <BR>

<UL>
 <LI><A HREF="#job"><IMG SRC="at_work.gif" ALT="My Job"
VSPACE=5 HSPACE=5 ALIGN=MIDDLE> My Job</A>

 <LI><A HREF="#books"><IMG SRC="books.gif" ALT="Books"
VSPACE=5 HSPACE=5 ALIGN=MIDDLE >
     Books I have Written</A>
</UL>

<H2><A NAME="job">Job</A> </H2>
My job keeps me very busy designing and tuning databases.

<H2> <A NAME="books"> Books </A> </H2>
In my spare time I have written books on a range of computer topics
and also a mountain bike trail guide.
</BODY>
</HTML>
```

Start the jump point

Define the graphic

End the jump point

Jump to here

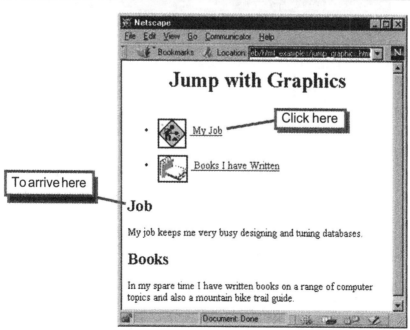

Click here

To arrive here

Image maps

How many times have you visited a Web site and been presented with a group of icons that you click on to go to different places in the site? The icons may be in a strip or a table, or integrated into a more free-form picture. If the icons load as a single image, the site is using an **image map**. Image maps offer precise control and the ability to navigate using shaped areas – rectangles, circles or polygons. This is a very friendly approach to use and makes it very easy for people to navigate your Web site.

A single Web document is not limited to one image map, therefore create as many as you require on a Web page. For example, an image map could be used at the top of the page for basic Web site navigation and further down in the document another image map provides access to more detailed information.

Image maps can be defined in two ways. The map definition can be written into the HTML page, alternatively, the definition can be stored with as a separate file and referenced from other pages. The later approach is for experts; in this book we will show you how to create a simple image map within an HTML document.

Image maps
at Amazon

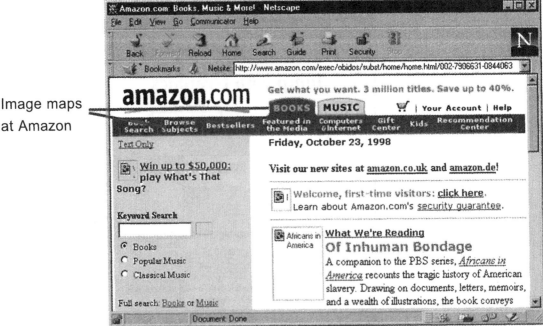

Using image maps

There are a number of steps to generating an image map. The only difficult one is describing the clickable area. The first step is to create the actual image, which can be achieved using your favourite graphics tool such as Paint Shop Pro. When complete, this image should be saved as a .GIF file.

Now each area that you want to be able to click on must be defined. There are three types of areas; rectangle, polygon and circle. A rectangle is defined by its coordinates measured in pixels; upper left x, upper left y, lower right x and lower left y. A polygon is represented by $x1$, $y2$, $x2$, $y2$ to xn, yn. Finally a circle is defined by the centre x,y coordinates and the radius. Some software tools are available to identify the coordinates, a good one is called MapEdit (see page 109). Alternatively, you can work them out yourself. Define the coordinates, good ones to start with are 0,0,50,50, and then display the HTML with the browser. Now run the mouse over the image map and note at which point the cursor changes to a hand, denoting a jump point. Continue to adjust the coordinates until this entire clickable area on the image map has a hand instead of a regular cursor. When you have the coordinates for the first clickable area, repeat the process for the next area.

The image map is included in the HTML document using two tags. First the **<IMG>** tag is used to define the actual image map using **SRC=** to define the actual image and the clause **USEMAP=** to point to the map definition and the clause **ISMAP** so that it knows that the graphic is an image map. Use the **Height=** and **Width=** clauses to control the size of the image map and the clause **border=0** to prevent a border being drawn around the image map.

Then the map is defined using the **<MAP>** tag. For each clickable area on the map use the tag **<AREA>**. Inside this tag you must state the shape of the area using the **SHAPE=** clause followed by the **COORD=** clause which specifies the actual area and then finally, define the point to jump to using the **HREF=** clause.

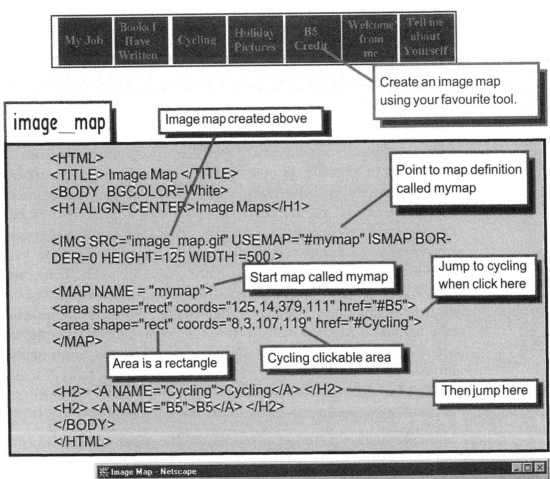

Create an image map using your favourite tool.

image__map

Image map created above

```
<HTML>
<TITLE> Image Map </TITLE>
<BODY  BGCOLOR=White>
<H1 ALIGN=CENTER>Image Maps</H1>

<IMG SRC="image_map.gif" USEMAP="#mymap" ISMAP BOR-
DER=0 HEIGHT=125 WIDTH =500 >

<MAP NAME = "mymap">
<area shape="rect" coords="125,14,379,111" href="#B5">
<area shape="rect" coords="8,3,107,119" href="#Cycling">
</MAP>

<H2> <A NAME="Cycling">Cycling</A> </H2>
<H2> <A NAME="B5">B5</A> </H2>
</BODY>
</HTML>
```

Point to map definition called mymap

Start map called mymap

Jump to cycling when click here

Area is a rectangle

Cycling clickable area

Then jump here

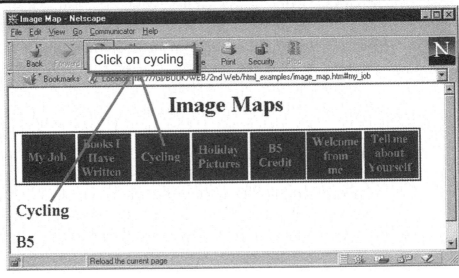

Click on cycling

Mapedit

Trying to create an image map using the trial and error method to determine the coordinates can be quite time-consuming. Therefore consider using a tool like MapEdit, which can be found at http://www.boutell.com/mapedit/. It is available for a 30 day trial and after that time it must be registered. Anyone who has to regularly create and maintain image maps will like this tool and some may consider it to be essential.

Unfortunately it doesn't get over the problem of first creating the image map, but once that is done, it will probably take you less than a minute or so to create the map.

When started, Mapedit asks for the HTML document and identifies which image to use from this file.

1   Using the mouse, identify each clickable area on the image. First click on the icon which corresponds to the type of area, e.g. rectangle, then click on the mouse to activate it, and drag the mouse across the area to create a box as illustrated in the example on the next page.

2   Click again to generate the box where you specify the URL.

3   Repeat this process for each clickable area and then save the HTML document. It will now be complete with a map definition.

Once the image map has been created, the next step is to create the HTML document into which the map definition is to be placed. It isn't necessary to use the actual HTML document, in fact it is probably safer to create a small HTML document into which the definition is saved and then the contents of this file are included in the actual document. As you can see from our example here, we started with very simple HTML that contains only the reference to the image map.

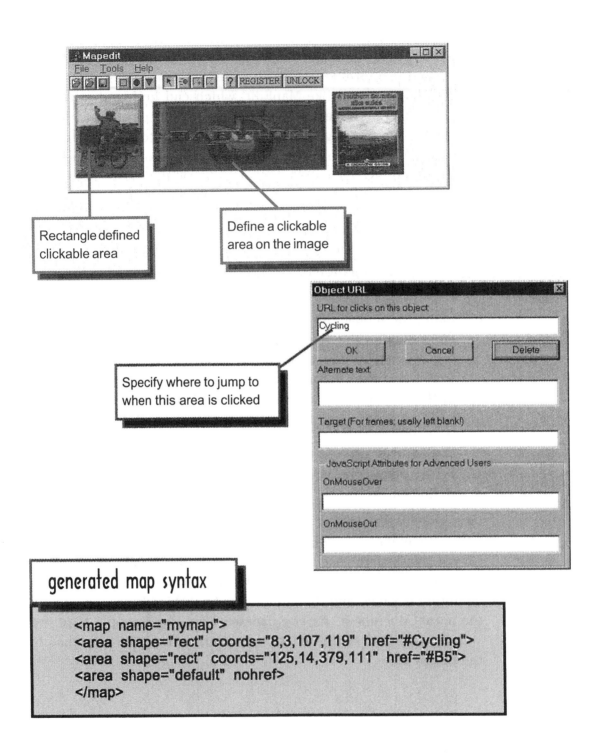

Rectangle defined clickable area

Define a clickable area on the image

Specify where to jump to when this area is clicked

generated map syntax

```
<map name="mymap">
<area shape="rect" coords="8,3,107,119" href="#Cycling">
<area shape="rect" coords="125,14,379,111" href="#B5">
<area shape="default" nohref>
</map>
```

Default style sheets

If your Web site comprised of 30+ pages, no Web designer would want to include the style sheet in every document. The solution to this problem, is a style sheet which we save once as HTML and then call it using the **<LINK>** tag in every document as illustrated below.

stylesheet.htm

Create the style sheet and store in its own HTML file

```
<HTML>
<STYLE>
    BODY {background-color:yellow}
    H1 {font: 22pt Courier; color:black}
    H2 {font: 18pt Times New Roman; color:blue; text-indent:25}
    P {font: 16pt Victorian; text-align: center; color: red}
    UL {list-style-type:square; color:red; font: 15pt Arial}
</STYLE>
</HTML>
```

style_def

Create the link to the stylesheet

```
<HTML>
<LINK  REL=STYLESHEET  HREF=stylesheet.htm >
<TITLE>Default Style sheet</TITLE>

<BODY>

    <H1>This is Black in Courier </H1>
    <H2> This is Blue and indented in slightly</H2>
    <P>This text should be red

    <UL>
        <LI>First list line with a square using Arial font
        <LI>second list line
    </UL>
</BODY>
</HTML>
```

Summary

In this chapter we have seen more techniques that can be used for creating links within a Web page, between the pages of your site and to pages on other sites elsewhere on the Web. These links can be created simply by attaching them to text or graphics.

Using image maps we can create a friendly environment and provide our visitor with an easy way to navigate our Web site. Simply click on an image which represents your area of interest.

If the same style is required on a set of pages, one style sheet can be linked by all pages.

Try creating some pages with links, using one or more of these techniques:

q   create several Web documents and then jump from one document to the next;

q   identify external Web sites that could be referenced from your Web site;

q   design different types of image maps and create the clickable areas.

6 Frames and forms

Frames 114

Simple frame 116

Frames and targets 120

Nested frames 122

Forms 124

mailto: me! 125

Simple form 126

More form options 128

Form created by FrontPage Express . 132

Summary 134

Frames

This feature is being used extensively, because it allows the screen to be split into various areas, each displaying its own information. Frames are used in many different ways and it's not everyone's Web site that needs them.

If we look at the Bike Nashbar Web site, we can see that they have several frames on their page. The top of the page contains static information; the frame on the left provides a list of manufacturers and the second frame a list of components. Selecting an item in either of those will replace the contents with a list of components and then the area that is currently displaying 'bike Nashbar' will change to a detailed description of the item you requested. This is a friendly way to display information and is very useful to catalogue publishers because it enables the readers to quickly review the items of interest.

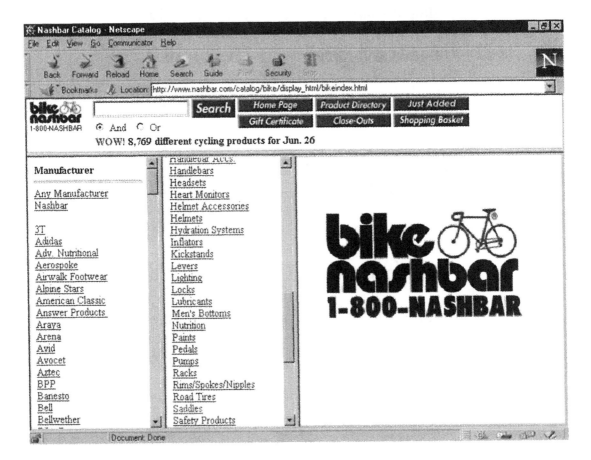

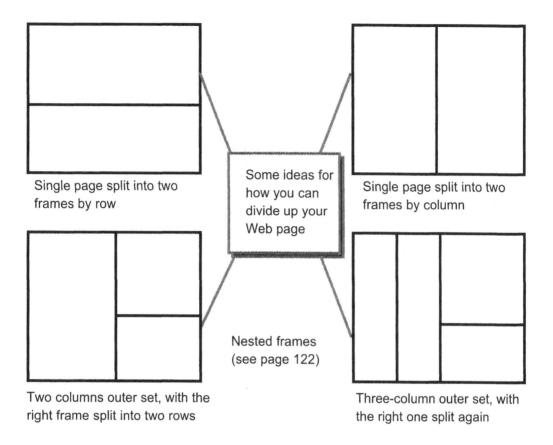

Single page split into two frames by row

Some ideas for how you can divide up your Web page

Single page split into two frames by column

Nested frames (see page 122)

Two columns outer set, with the right frame split into two rows

Three-column outer set, with the right one split again

Frames can be used in a number of ways to divide our Web page into multiple areas and shown above are a few examples of what is possible. One important point to remember about frames is that the reader doesn't need to be aware of them. They can be extremely useful for keeping important parts of the Web page, such as navigation bars, permanently visible.

Here is an example of a navigation bar, now imagine keeping that in a frame at the bottom of every Web page so that you could visit anywhere on the Web site.

1-800-727-NOVA	FAX:(520)292-9852	staff@novaspace.com	*non-U.S.*	Visit our gallery
	Original Paintings	Limited Editions	Collector's Exchange	Astronaut Autographs
	Digital Editions	Posters	Cards & Miniatures	Screen Savers	Books	Meteorites
HOME	Our Catalog	On Sale	Calendar	View by Artist	Ordering info
What's New	*Contest*	*Feedback*	*Search*	*FAQ*	*Hot Links*	*Teachers*	*Dealers*

Simple frame

The first example is a simple document comprised of two frames and display some of the HTML documents that we have already seen inside those frames. This is the first time that we have been able to include the source from more than one HTML document on a single page. The browser will automatically adjust the windows and create scroll bars to accommodate the HTML document.

A number of tags are required to define a frame.

<FRAMESET>

The frame is defined using the **<FRAMESET>** tag and is closed with a **</FRAMESET>**. To create a frame that divides the page horizontally, then the qualifier **ROWS=** is used and for a frame which divides the page vertically, use **COLS=**.

The size of each frame can be set by specifying its size in pixels or as a percentage of the total size, or we can use an asterisk, which tells the browser to match the size to the remaining space. Therefore, to create two frames of equal size that span the rows, you would enter **ROWS="*,*"**. To create a document that comprises of three column frames, where the first frame takes the default size, the second frame is 25% of the document size and the third frame is 200 pixels, the tag would be written as **<FRAMESET COLS= "*,25%,200">**.

More complex frames, which span rows and columns are created by nesting the <FRAMESET> tags.

Although it is possible to create a document that comprises of many frames, in practice, you will usually only want two or maybe three because otherwise the text or graphics may be difficult to read.

<FRAME>

Once the number of frames have been defined, the specifics for each frame are defined using the **<FRAME>** tag. This has no closing tag. There is a <FRAME> tag for every framed area on the document. Inside it, each frame is given a name, using the **NAME=** clause. It is advisable to choose a name that is easily remembered, because it is this frame name that is used to tell HTML into which frame a document is to be displayed.

If the frame is to immediately include some HTML source, then this is achieved using the **SRC=** clause. In our examples overleaf, we can see that as the Web page displays the frame, it automatically includes the documents that we have specified.

If you are going to display into a frame later, then you may prefer to start by displaying a blank source document, so that every frame appears identical. Otherwise you could end up with the default background of grey which may spoil the look of your Web page.

\<NOFRAME\>

It is also worth considering that not everybody may be using a browser that supports frames. Therefore, they would not be able to see the content of your Web page. To overcome this problem, use the <NOFRAME> tag.

Between the <NOFRAME> and </NOFRAME> tag, specify the HTML that is to be displayed and this will appear instead of the HTML between the <FRAMESET> tags.

It is probably wise to include only basic HTML and avoid special features like image maps and other extensions, so that you can be sure that the visitor will be able to see your Web page.

Tip

If the frames will not display using your browser then verify that the version of your browser supports frames.

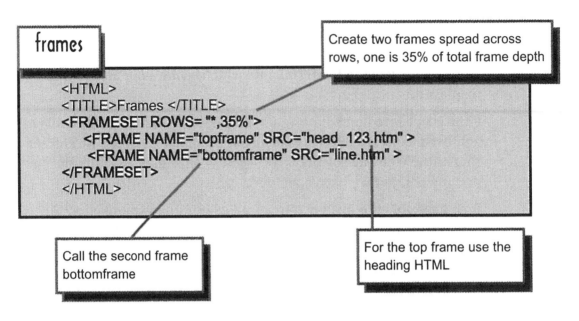

frames

Create two frames spread across rows, one is 35% of total frame depth

```
<HTML>
<TITLE>Frames </TITLE>
<FRAMESET ROWS= "*,35%">
    <FRAME NAME="topframe" SRC="head_123.htm" >
    <FRAME NAME="bottomframe" SRC="line.htm" >
</FRAMESET>
</HTML>
```

Call the second frame bottomframe

For the top frame use the heading HTML

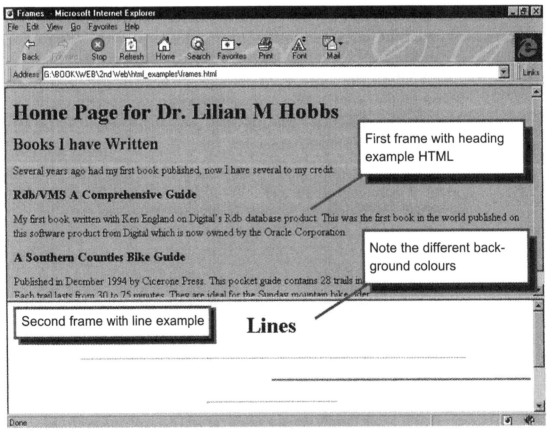

Frames - Microsoft Internet Explorer

File Edit View Go Favorites Help

Back Forward Stop Refresh Home Search Favorites Print Font Mail

Address G:\BOOK\WEB\2nd Web\html_examples\frames.html

Home Page for Dr. Lilian M Hobbs

Books I have Written

Several years ago had my first book published, now I have several to my credit.

Rdb/VMS A Comprehensive Guide

My first book written with Ken England on Digital's Rdb database product. This was the first book in the world published on this software product from Digital which is now owned by the Oracle Corporation.

A Southern Counties Bike Guide

Published in Decmber 1994 by Cicerone Press. This pocket guide contains 28 trails in Each trail lasts from 30 to 75 minutes. They are ideal for the Sunday mountain bike rider

First frame with heading example HTML

Note the different background colours

Second frame with line example

Lines

Done

118

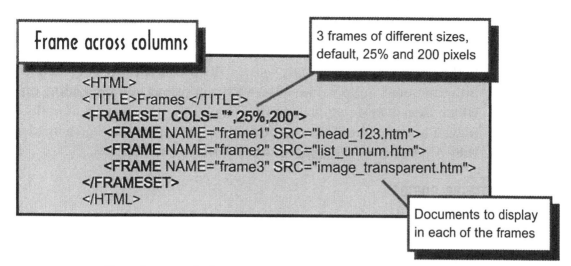

Frame across columns

3 frames of different sizes, default, 25% and 200 pixels

```
<HTML>
<TITLE>Frames </TITLE>
<FRAMESET COLS= "*,25%,200">
    <FRAME NAME="frame1" SRC="head_123.htm">
    <FRAME NAME="frame2" SRC="list_unnum.htm">
    <FRAME NAME="frame3" SRC="image_transparent.htm">
</FRAMESET>
</HTML>
```

Documents to display in each of the frames

Note how each frame is its own Web document, which means it can use different fonts, background colours and image and of course content.

Here you can see that using more than 3 frames would only provide a limited text area.

Three frames divided by columns

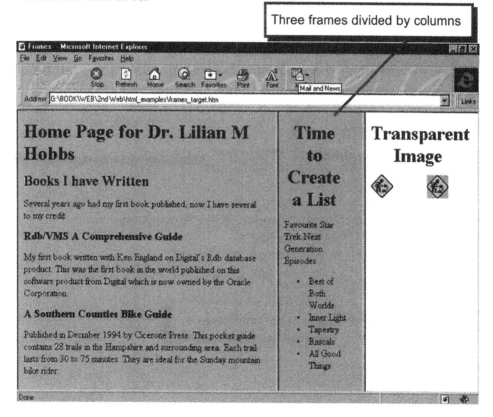

Frames and targets

In the previous example, only one HTML document was ever loaded into the frame. Suppose we have a list of options and depending on which item is selected, determines the HTML document that is displayed in the frame. This can be achieved using a new clause inside the <A> tag where the hyperlink is defined, called target=.

Target = <frame name>

The first step is to create an HTML document that defines the frames. In the example here we have created three frames and called them frame1, frame2 and frame3. frame1 will be used to display the HTML document called framet1.htm (which is the source shown opposite with the hyperlinks).

Inside the HTML document framet1.htm, we include a **Target=** clause in the **<A>** tags and there we specify the names of the frame where the linked documents are to be displayed. Don't forget to include the **HREF=** clause to specify which HTML document to use.

Alternatively the **Target** clause can contain the keywords; **_blank** will load into a new window, **_parent** into the parent window and **_self** into the same window.

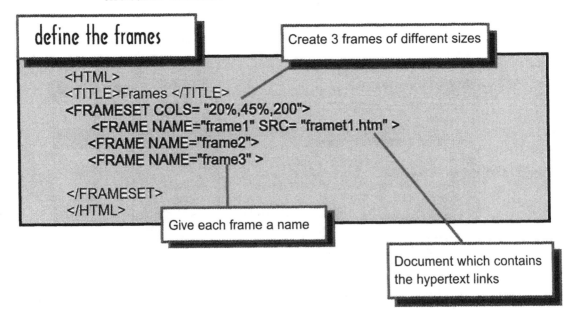

define the frames

Create 3 frames of different sizes

```
<HTML>
<TITLE>Frames </TITLE>
<FRAMESET COLS= "20%,45%,200">
    <FRAME NAME="frame1" SRC= "framet1.htm" >
    <FRAME NAME="frame2">
    <FRAME NAME="frame3" >

</FRAMESET>
</HTML>
```

Give each frame a name

Document which contains the hypertext links

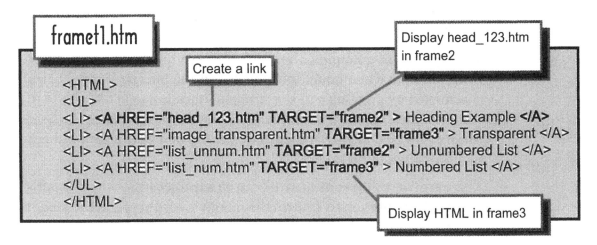

```
<HTML>
<UL>
<LI> <A HREF="head_123.htm" TARGET="frame2" > Heading Example </A>
<LI> <A HREF="image_transparent.htm" TARGET="frame3" > Transparent </A>
<LI> <A HREF="list_unnum.htm" TARGET="frame2" > Unnumbered List </A>
<LI> <A HREF="list_num.htm" TARGET="frame3" > Numbered List </A>
</UL>
</HTML>
```

In framet1.htm an unnumbered list is defined. The first entry states that when you click *heading example*, the document head_123.htm, will be displayed in frame2. Each entry in the list, is similarly assigned a frame where its source is displayed.

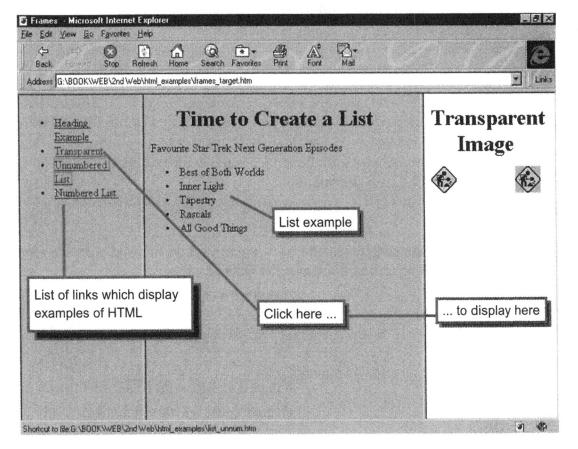

Nested frames

In the previous examples, the frames have either be in columns or rows, but what if a combination of rows and columns is required? This is achieved by creating a nested frame. This is a useful technique to learn, because nested frames enabled you to create Web pages where there could be a standard banner at the top and bottom and frames of information in between.

There are some other options that can be specified inside the **<FRAME>** tag which enable you to control the margins, scrolling and the size of the frame.

Margins

The height and width of the margin in pixels can be specified using the **MARGINHEIGHT=** and **MARGINWIDTH=** clauses respectively. Choose a low value if you want the frame to be invisible or high if a distinctive border between the frames is needed.

Scrolling

By default, a frame is created with scroll bars, which will appear if the document cannot be fully displayed in the frame. To turn this feature off, you must specify **SCROLLING=NO**. However, use this option only if the text fits exactly in the box, otherwise the reader will not be able to see all of the information.

Change frame size

If you want to prevent the user from resizing the frame, this can be enabled by adding the clause **NORESIZE** to the <FRAME> tag.

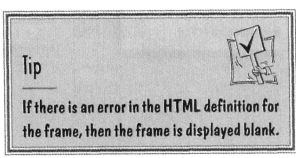

Tip

If there is an error in the HTML definition for the frame, then the frame is displayed blank.

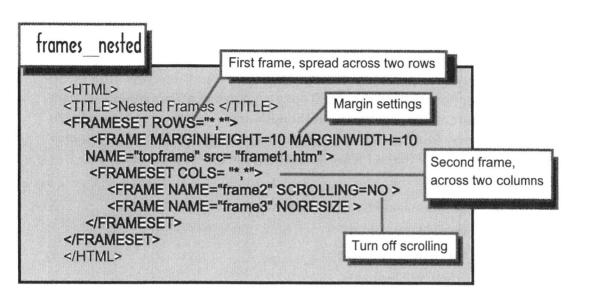

frames_nested

First frame, spread across two rows

Margin settings

```
<HTML>
<TITLE>Nested Frames </TITLE>
<FRAMESET ROWS="*,*">
    <FRAME MARGINHEIGHT=10 MARGINWIDTH=10
    NAME="topframe" src= "framet1.htm" >
    <FRAMESET COLS= "*,*">
        <FRAME NAME="frame2" SCROLLING=NO >
        <FRAME NAME="frame3" NORESIZE >
    </FRAMESET>
</FRAMESET>
</HTML>
```

Second frame, across two columns

Turn off scrolling

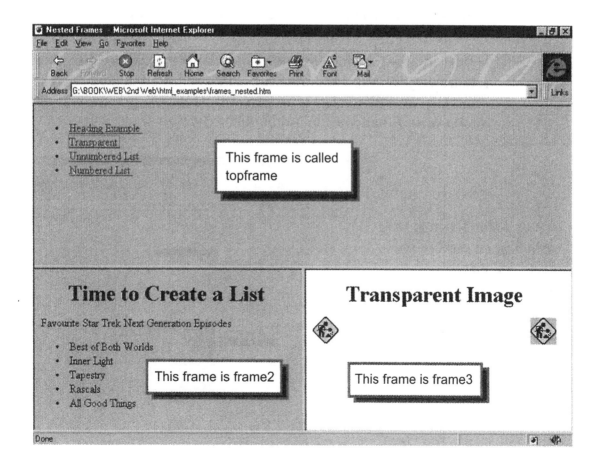

This frame is called topframe

This frame is frame2

This frame is frame3

Forms

Initially Web pages provided information and there was little or no interaction with the reader. Today, visitors to a Web site will expect to interact with it and one method for achieving this is to use a form. This may look just like a paper form, or on some Web sites you may not be aware that a form is being completed. Typical uses are:

- surveys
- quotations, such as car insurance
- ordering a product
- searching a Web site
- providing feedback

Forms can also be used to obtain feedback such as comments. For some reason, it seems that people would rather complete a form than send e-mail to a complete stranger. With a form, they don't have to think, just answer the questions

Forms are ideal to include on a personal Web page because they require very little space. Forms, like tables require a number of tags. Therefore, considering using a tool like Front Page Express which has a form wizard that you can use to define the form.

A form doesn't have to only accept typed data. At the Exchange & Mart site, you don't have to key in anything, instead you select from the two drop-down lists and then click on the button to send.

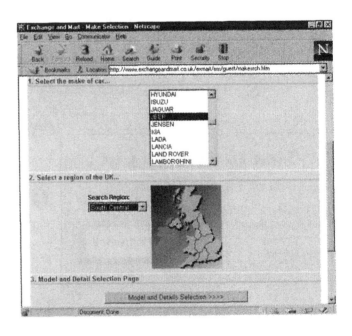

mailto: me!

Before we go any further into forms, we should look at this technique that allows a visitor to your Web page to communicate with you via e-mail. On your page you can display an icon or text which when the visitor clicks on, will automatically display their e-mail software with your address already completed. They simply enter their text and then send the message. A variation on this technique can be used to send to you the information that a visitor enters into a form.

<A HREF=mailto: >

To send mail to yourself, use the **<A HREF = mailto:** tag followed by your e-mail address. Add some text or an icon so that people know they will be mailing you. Finally close the tag with **</A>**. Therefore to send e-mail to the author

<A HREF="mailto:lmhobbs@clara.net"> Mail me </A>

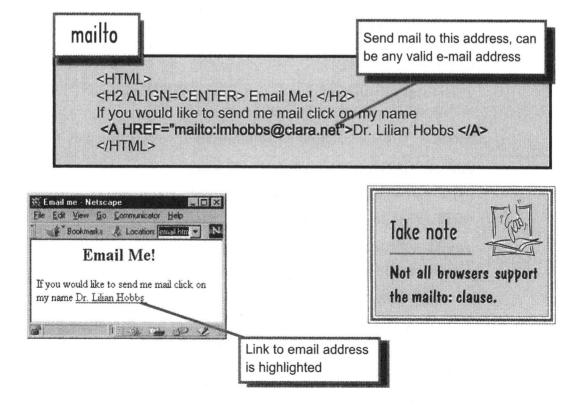

mailto

Send mail to this address, can be any valid e-mail address

```
<HTML>
<H2 ALIGN=CENTER> Email Me! </H2>
If you would like to send me mail click on my name
 <A HREF="mailto:lmhobbs@clara.net">Dr. Lilian Hobbs </A>
</HTML>
```

Email me - Netscape
File Edit View Go Communicator Help
Bookmarks Location email.html

Email Me!

If you would like to send me mail click on my name Dr. Lilian Hobbs

Link to email address is highlighted

Take note

Not all browsers support the mailto: clause.

125

Simple form

A form can be defined anywhere in the HTML document. When defining forms, the <PRE> tag is sometimes very useful, to explicitly state how the text is to be displayed.

<FORM>

The form is defined with the **<FORM>** tag. Inside the tag you must say how you want the contents of the form to be sent to you. The recommended method is to have it sent by e-mail which is achieved by adding to the tag the parameter **METHOD=POST** and then **ACTION=** to advise what to do with the data just received. Usually the ACTION= would point to a URL for a cgi script or if you wanted to send it via email it would be ACTION= "mailto:your e-mail address"   Therefore to send a form to the author the tag would be

     <FORM METHOD=POST ACTION="mailto:lmhobbs@clara.net" >

<INPUT>

To input information into the form, first some text is required to tell the reader what to input. This is achieved as if we were writing any text in HTML.

Then to specify the input field, use the tag **<INPUT>** followed by some of these clauses inside the tag.

NAME= " " to give each piece of information you enter a name

SIZE= to specify the size of the input string

SRC= if an image is to be associated with the input area

TYPE=TEXT for a text field

ALIGN= for the position of the field. Therefore to define an input field for a name that is 40 characters wide would be:

     <INPUT NAME="yourname" SIZE=40 >

The <INPUT> tag has over a dozen different clauses which may be specified and we will see some of these options on the following pages.

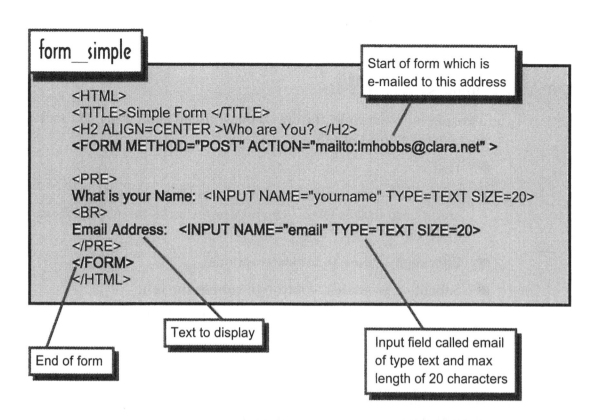

form_simple

Start of form which is e-mailed to this address

```
<HTML>
<TITLE>Simple Form </TITLE>
<H2 ALIGN=CENTER >Who are You? </H2>
<FORM METHOD="POST" ACTION="mailto:lmhobbs@clara.net" >

<PRE>
What is your Name:  <INPUT NAME="yourname" TYPE=TEXT SIZE=20>
<BR>
Email Address:   <INPUT NAME="email" TYPE=TEXT SIZE=20>
</PRE>
</FORM>
</HTML>
```

Text to display

End of form

Input field called email of type text and max length of 20 characters

Tip

You can test the layout of your form without connecting to your Internet service. But to test receiving form submissions, you will have to connect to your Internet service, enter data and submit the form.

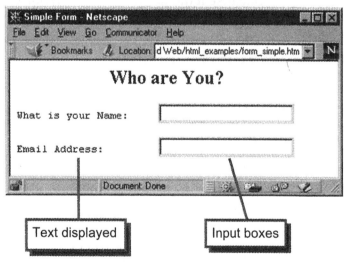

Text displayed

Input boxes

127

More form options

Form Control using <INPUT TYPE=>

In the previous example, the only data we could input was text, but it can take the following values:

- **Text**

- **Password** — typed text is hidden, ideal for passwords or credit card details which you may not want to be displayed on a screen

- **Checkbox** — used to indicate options

- **Submit** — generates a button to submit the form

- **Reset** — generates a reset button to clear the form

- **File** — can upload a file

- **Image** — same as **Submit** but uses an image for button

The form on the previous page would never have been sent to anyone because it did not have a **Submit** button which is created using **TYPE= "Submit"**, It is always a good idea to include on your form a clear button via the **TYPE= "Reset"**, just in case someone makes a mistake.

<TEXT AREA>

To create a multi-line area to input text you can use the tag called **<TEXT AREA>**. Inside this tag, specify **NAME=** for the field name and then how many **ROWS=** in the text field, followed by how many **COLUMNS=** are required. This is closed with the tag **</TEXTAREA>**. Therefore to create a comment area, into a field called comments, which has 5 rows of 40 columns, the tag would be as follows:

<TEXTAREA NAME= "comments" ROWS=5 COLS=40 >

If you create several text areas on your form, the tab order can be controlled by adding the clause **TABINDEX=** to this tag.

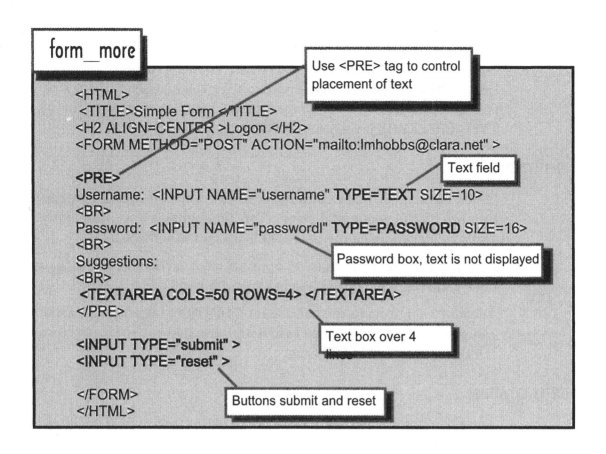

```
<HTML>
 <TITLE>Simple Form </TITLE>
<H2 ALIGN=CENTER >Logon </H2>
<FORM METHOD="POST" ACTION="mailto:lmhobbs@clara.net" >

<PRE>
Username:  <INPUT NAME="username" TYPE=TEXT SIZE=10>
<BR>
Password:  <INPUT NAME="passwordl" TYPE=PASSWORD SIZE=16>
<BR>
Suggestions:
<BR>
 <TEXTAREA COLS=50 ROWS=4> </TEXTAREA>
</PRE>

<INPUT TYPE="submit" >
<INPUT TYPE="reset" >

</FORM>
</HTML>
```

Use <PRE> tag to control placement of text

Text field

Password box, text is not displayed

Text box over 4 lines

Buttons submit and reset

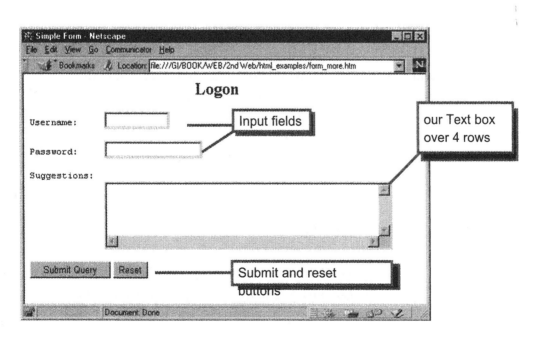

Input fields

our Text box over 4 rows

Submit and reset buttons

Checkboxes

Checkboxes are extremely useful when asking a reader questions. Rather than struggling to type in text, they can click on the box that is appropriate to them. To create a checkbox use the clause **TYPE=CHECKBOX** inside the **<INPUT >** tag.

Select from a list

In one of the previous examples we saw a drop-down list of entries from which the user could select. This technique is used frequently and is achieved using the tags **<SELECT>** and **<OPTION>**.

First give the <SELECT> tag with optional clauses **NAME=** and **SIZE=** to determine the number of choices the reader will see.

Then for each item in the list use the **<OPTION>** tag with a **VALUE=** clause with the value and text associated with that value. Finally close the list with the **</SELECT>** tag.

Limits on values

There are times when you want to control the value a field may take. This is possible by adding the clause **MIN=** and **MAX=** and a **TYPE=RANGE** to the **<INPUT>** tag.

Behind the scenes

When you press the submit button what actually takes place? The contents of your form are sent to the place specified by the **ACTION=** clause inside the <FORM> tag which is usually a CGI script. The CGI program processes the information received and then passes back the results to the browser that sent them as an HTML document.

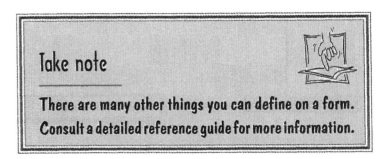

Take note

There are many other things you can define on a form. Consult a detailed reference guide for more information.

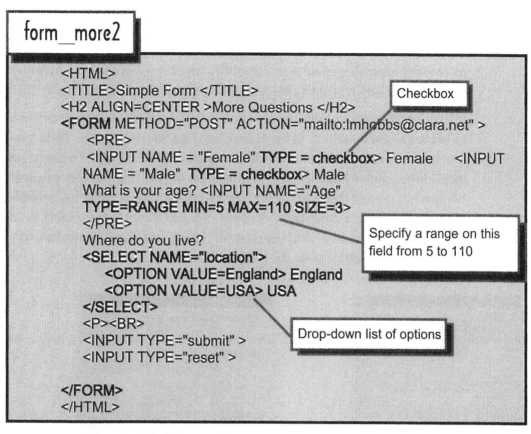

```
<HTML>
<TITLE>Simple Form </TITLE>
<H2 ALIGN=CENTER >More Questions </H2>
<FORM METHOD="POST" ACTION="mailto:lmhobbs@clara.net" >
    <PRE>
    <INPUT NAME = "Female" TYPE = checkbox> Female    <INPUT
    NAME = "Male" TYPE = checkbox> Male
    What is your age? <INPUT NAME="Age"
    TYPE=RANGE MIN=5 MAX=110 SIZE=3>
    </PRE>
    Where do you live?
    <SELECT NAME="location">
        <OPTION VALUE=England> England
        <OPTION VALUE=USA> USA
    </SELECT>
    <P><BR>
    <INPUT TYPE="submit" >
    <INPUT TYPE="reset" >

</FORM>
</HTML>
```

Checkbox

Specify a range on this field from 5 to 110

Drop-down list of options

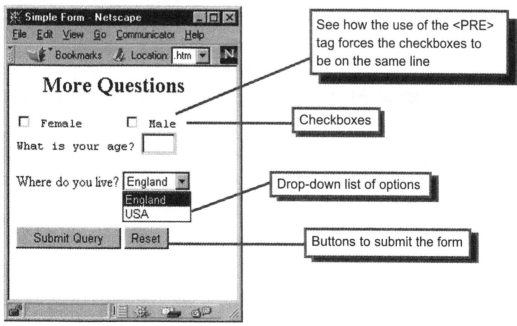

See how the use of the <PRE> tag forces the checkboxes to be on the same line

Checkboxes

Drop-down list of options

Buttons to submit the form

Form created by FrontPage Express

Microsoft FrontPage Express simplifies the job of creating a form by providing a wizard that takes you through all the steps.

It begins by asking you to name the form document and to provide a title for the form, which is displayed at the top of the page. Next you select the type of information that you would like people to enter on your form. FrontPage offers a number of choices, which is nice, because it means that you don't have to think about what to include. In this example we selected Personal details. Now that doesn't mean that you have to have all those fields, because the next window asks you to select which ones are required.

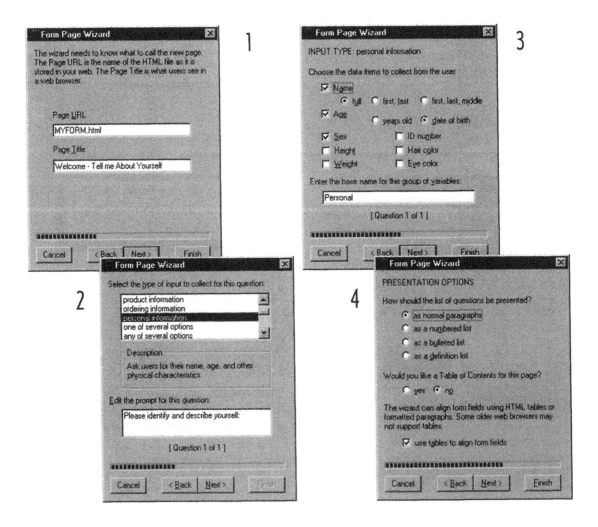

Once all the fields on the form have been selected, it asks you how you would like them presented, such as in a list, or as in our example, using ordinary paragraphs. At the bottom of each window on the wizard, you may have noticed a rectangular box that is starting to fill up, rather like a gauge. The purpose of this is to let you know how far through the wizard process you are.

When you click on the *Finish* button, the form then appears in the main FrontPage Express window. Don't forget that you can then customise the form to your own requirements before you save it.

By default all pages are created with a grey background but most people change this colour. To do this, click on *Format* on the strip menu and then select *Background*.

Summary

The use of frames enables the screen to be split in such a way that different types of information can be displayed. This technique is often used on Web sites where you can place orders, simply select from the left and see the detail on the right.

So far all the techniques we have seen have involved the visitor to our Web site, reading and clicking on areas to obtain information. Now we have learnt some techniques that enables us to interact with the visitor. Using a form we can interact with people and obtain information. This could be as simple as finding out who visited our page to receive an order for goods that a company sells.

Useful techniques to practise would be:

❑ investigate the use of frames and determine whether horizontal or vertical frames are best for your Web site;

❑ create some forms, experimenting with the different options and understand how to interpret the results when they are sent back to you.

Take note

The responses from forms are sent back encoded, so it's a little tricky to read, but by no means impossible. If you plan to do anything serious with forms then another component is required to handle the data, which is called CGI which stands for Common Gateway Interface. A CGI program may have already have been written to perform the task that you need, otherwise you will have to write your own CGI scripts and many books have been written on this subject.

7 Active content

What is sound? 136

Including sound 138

Background sound 140

Including video 142

Scrolling message 144

Counters 146

Java 148

Javascript 154

Summary 158

What is sound?

Probably the first thing you do when you meet someone is say 'Hello'. Therefore, why shouldn't a visitor to your web site be greeted with a welcome or music. For instance, visit the Chrysler corporation web site at www.chryslercars.com and you will hear some nice music.

Using sound is not difficult, yet few sites implement it on their web page. Many commercial sites are now realising the potential of communication by sound so that instead of seeing the text of an interview, – which they would probably not read in its entirety — Web site visitors can listen to someone's voice and have the benefit of hearing the tones and accents in it. For example, at the World Wrestling Federation site, you can hear the news for the last four weeks.

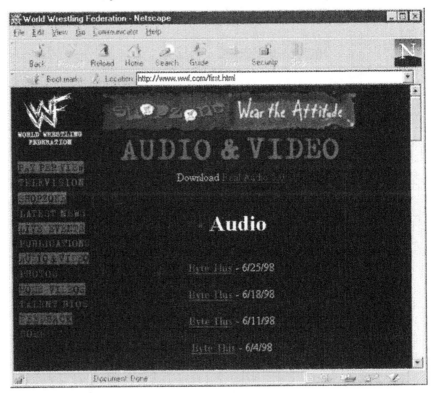

All that is required to listen to a sound file is a sound card, speakers or headphones and a browser configured to play the file. Like pictures, sound is stored on a computer in several different formats, the most popular of which is .**WAV**.

Many sites make use of the Real Audio browser plug-in, which allows you to start listening to the sound file before it has been received in its entirety. As the data is received, it is played back, and provided there are no data transfer problems, the music or other sound should be heard without interruptions. To create this type of file you will have to purchase some software which can be ordered at www.real.com.

Here we can see an the Real Audio software in use

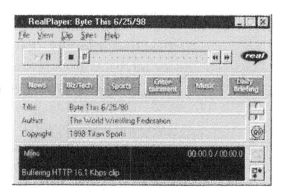

Configuring the browser

To play sound your browser must be configured to start the software that plays that file. For example, a .WAV file can be played by:

● Media Player supplied with Windows;

● Soundo'LE in Soundblaster cards;

Every browser is configured slightly differently, but you will usually find it under a section called Options or Preferences. Here it will list the different file types such as .WAV and you specify which program is to run when this file type is encountered by your browser.

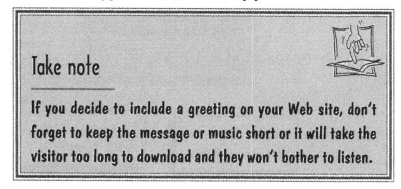

Take note

If you decide to include a greeting on your Web site, don't forget to keep the message or music short or it will take the visitor too long to download and they won't bother to listen.

Including sound

Including sound on your Web page is very easy provided you have:

- **sound card**
- **microphone** plugged into the *mic* socket on the sound card

The first step is to create the sound file which can be created using tools such as the Windows utility **Sound Recorder**.

Making a sound file

First start the utility that will record the sound, such as **Sound Recorder**. If it is already running, use the File – New command to startt a new file. When you are ready to speak, press the red record button on the right-hand side. It will now start recording and you can tell that it is picking up your voice because the flat wave sign will increase in height. When you have finished, press the stop button. Then to check what has been recorded, press the play button and enjoy the sound of your own voice. Now save the file as a .WAV type.

One important point to remember, is to make sure that the sound file is stored in the same folder as the HTML document that you are reading, otherwise the browser will not be able to find the file to play it. Once you have a sound file, it is included on your Web page using the <A> tag.

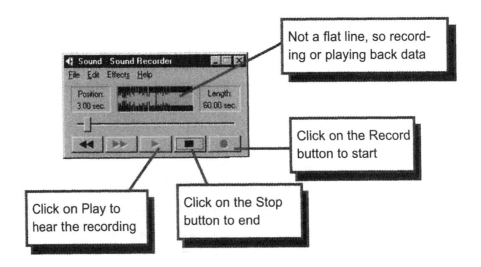

Not a flat line, so recording or playing back data

Click on the Record button to start

Click on Play to hear the recording

Click on the Stop button to end

Sound Source <A HREF= >

A sound file is included by specifying its name within the **<A HREF=>** tag. It is the same process that we saw for defining a jump point, except that this time, an actual filename is held within the quotes. Don't forget to close the tag with </A>.

Next to the tag it is a good idea to specify some text to describe what the sound file contains and to advise on its size.

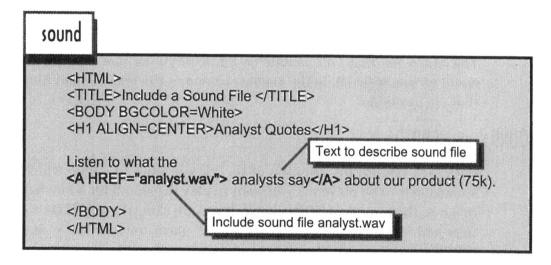

```
sound

<HTML>
<TITLE>Include a Sound File </TITLE>
<BODY BGCOLOR=White>
<H1 ALIGN=CENTER>Analyst Quotes</H1>

Listen to what the                      Text to describe sound file
<A HREF="analyst.wav"> analysts say</A> about our product (75k).

</BODY>                  Include sound file analyst.wav
</HTML>
```

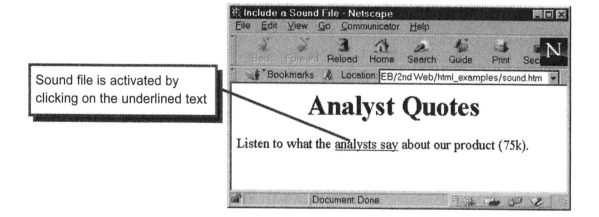

Sound file is activated by clicking on the underlined text

Analyst Quotes

Listen to what the analysts say about our product (75k).

Background sound

Now that you know how to include a sound file on a Web page, you could select one to load automatically, although you must be careful to choose a sound file that doesn't require too much space, because otherwise it will significantly increase the time required to load your Web page.

Sounds can be embedded into the background of a page using special tags. Internet Explorer 4 responds to the <BGSOUND> tag. The equivalent for Netscape browsers is the <EMBED> tag.

The sound file that you include could be anything that you like. It could be you welcoming the reader, or one of the many sound files that are available.

<BGSOUND> or <EMBED>

Both tags require the addition of the clause **SRC=** to define which sound file is to be played. If you want to play the sound file a number of times, then add the **LOOP=** clause. If you are using the <EMBED> tag then add **AUTOSTART=TRUE** so that it plays automatically and **HIDDEN=TRUE** so that the player software is not visible. One point to bear in mind is that when the browser processes the HTML, nothing will appear on the web page to indicate that a sound file is being played, that is, it is completely transparent to the surfer.

If you are looking for some places on the Internet to find some sound files then take a look at these sites:

http://earthstation1.simplenet.com/homepage.html

http://www.soundamerica.com/

http://www.whoopie.com/

http://www.dailywav.com/

http://www.slonet.org/~rloomis/

Tip

MIDI files are the most compact form of music files, but you need special software to create them.

140

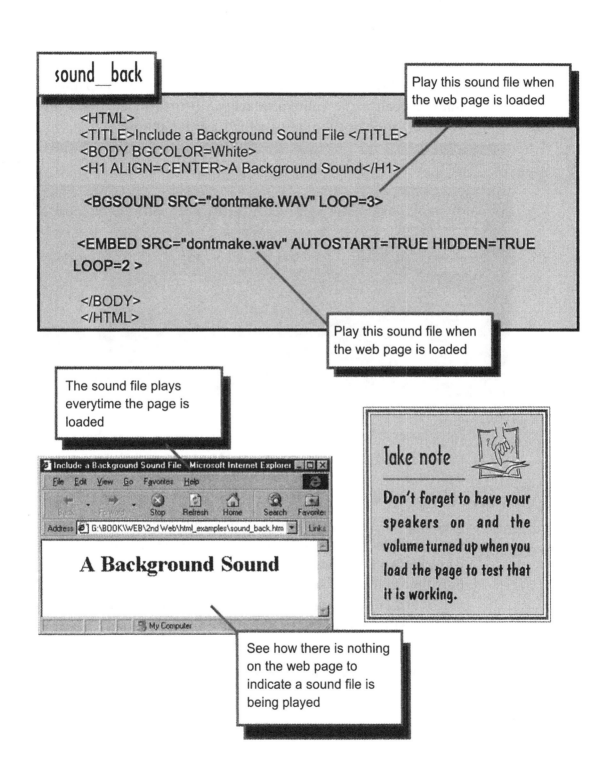

sound__back

```
<HTML>
<TITLE>Include a Background Sound File </TITLE>
<BODY BGCOLOR=White>
<H1 ALIGN=CENTER>A Background Sound</H1>

<BGSOUND SRC="dontmake.WAV" LOOP=3>

<EMBED SRC="dontmake.wav" AUTOSTART=TRUE HIDDEN=TRUE
LOOP=2 >

</BODY>
</HTML>
```

Play this sound file when the web page is loaded

Play this sound file when the web page is loaded

The sound file plays everytime the page is loaded

Include a Background Sound File - Microsoft Internet Explorer

File   Edit   View   Go   Favorites   Help

Back   Forward   Stop   Refresh   Home   Search   Favorites

Address   G:\BOOK\WEB\2nd Web\html_examples\sound_back.htm   Links

A Background Sound

My Computer

Take note

Don't forget to have your speakers on and the volume turned up when you load the page to test that it is working.

See how there is nothing on the web page to indicate a sound file is being played

Including video

An increasing number of sites on the Web provide videos for the reader to download and play. The TV and movie companies were quick to realise the value of placing a promotional trailer for this week's episode or their latest movie, on the Internet.

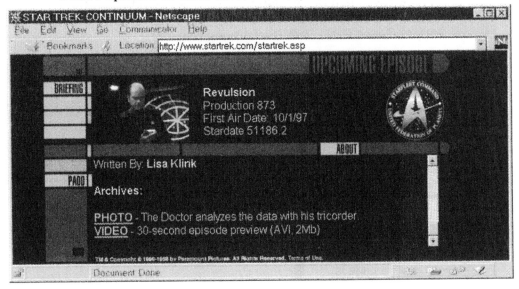

On personal Web sites, video is not usually found because until recently, video files were expensive to create and storage space was limited. Now with service providers offering 25Mb of storage space, video is feasible.

Creating the video itself, is now possible because video cards are readily available which capture video from a camcorder, TV or video. If you know that in the future you would like to work with video, then next time you select a graphics card, choose one that has an add-on video card. For example, cards from manufacturer Matrox are designed to work with their Rainbow Runner studio card.

The file types that are usually used for video files is Video for Windows .AVI and Quicktime which has an extension of .MOV.

Video Source <A HREF= >

A video file is included using the same technique as per a sound file. Specify the name of the video file within the **<A HREF= " ">** tag. It is the same process as for defining a jump point, except that this time, an actual filename is held within the quotes. Don't forget to close the tag with </A>.

Next to the tag write text to describe what the video file contains and its size, so that a visitor can decide whether or not to download it.

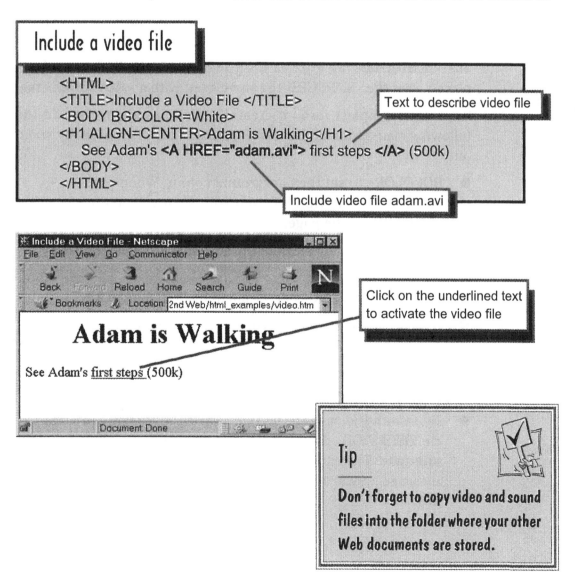

Include a video file

```
<HTML>
<TITLE>Include a Video File </TITLE>
<BODY BGCOLOR=White>
<H1 ALIGN=CENTER>Adam is Walking</H1>
     See Adam's <A HREF="adam.avi"> first steps </A> (500k)
</BODY>
</HTML>
```

Text to describe video file

Include video file adam.avi

Click on the underlined text to activate the video file

Adam is Walking

See Adam's first steps (500k)

Tip

Don't forget to copy video and sound files into the folder where your other Web documents are stored.

Scrolling message

Have you ever visited a Web site and seen a scrolling message and thought to yourself that you would like to include that on your site? Later we will meet Java and JavaScript, and most sites that have a scrolling message use one of these to perform the task.

The good news is that all is not lost becausethere is a tag which will create a scrolling message, though it only works when the page is viewed in Internet Explorer.

<MARQUEE>

The **<MARQUEE>** tag creates a scrolling message. The message is placed after the <MARQUEE> tag and closed with a **</MARQUEE>** tag.

Used in its simplest form, it creates a plain message, But add the following clauses inside the <MARQUEE> tag and it will really stand out.

- **BGCOLOR=** to set the background colour. When used in conjunction with HEIGHT= and WIDTH= it will create a box that stands out on the page.

- Set the height and width of the scrolling are using **HEIGHT=** and **WIDTH=** .

- The scrolling speed is determined by **SCROLLAMOUNT=** .

- By default the message scrolls from the left side to the right side. You can change this using the **DIRECTION=** clause.

- To control how many times the message loops around using **LOOP=** .

- By default the message scrolls across the screen, but using the **BEHAVIOR=** clause you can specify **slide**, **scroll** or **alternate**. The example here uses **alternate** which males the message appear to bounce back and forth within the defined area.

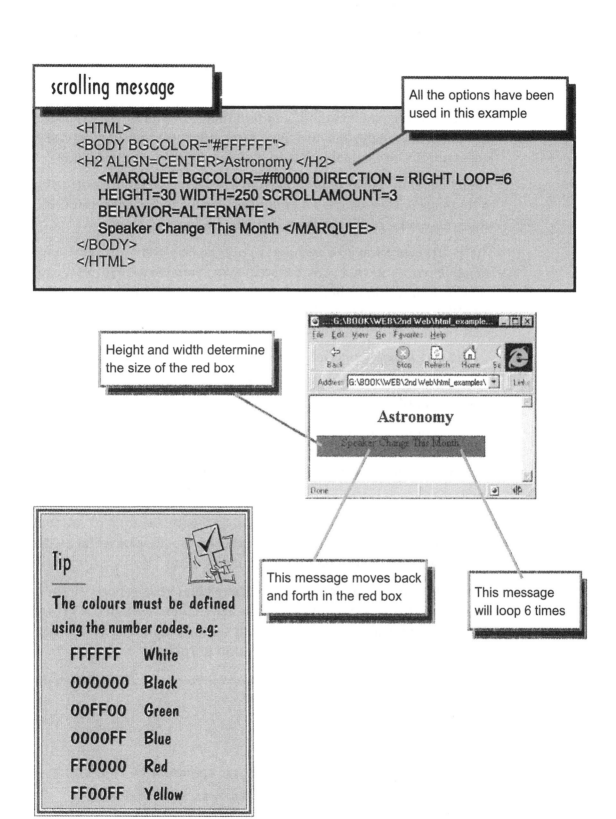

scrolling message

All the options have been used in this example

```
<HTML>
<BODY BGCOLOR="#FFFFFF">
<H2 ALIGN=CENTER>Astronomy </H2>
    <MARQUEE BGCOLOR=#ff0000 DIRECTION = RIGHT LOOP=6
    HEIGHT=30 WIDTH=250 SCROLLAMOUNT=3
    BEHAVIOR=ALTERNATE >
    Speaker Change This Month </MARQUEE>
</BODY>
</HTML>
```

Height and width determine the size of the red box

Astronomy

Speaker Change This Month

This message moves back and forth in the red box

This message will loop 6 times

Tip

The colours must be defined using the number codes, e.g:

FFFFFF	White
000000	Black
00FF00	Green
0000FF	Blue
FF0000	Red
FF00FF	Yellow

Counters

Once a Web page is installed, you don't know if anybody is visiting your page. Although you may have a form, not every visitor will reply. The solution to this problem is to install a counter on your page.

When you reference a counter on your Web page, the number of visits to the page will be held on a computer somewhere on the Internet, which may slow down the time required to display the page.

There are many ways to include a counter on your Web page and hopefully your Internet provider will make available a script that you can use. If they don't, then a good site to visit where you can register your Web page and where they provide clear and easy instructions on what to include in your HTML document is:

    http://www.digits.com/web_counter/

This site will even let you choose the type of counter you want to display and the starting number.

Using a counter normally involves calling a CGI script, which is a program that runs on the server. To use the one at Claranet you would specify the following in your HTML document.

    <IMG SRC="/cgi-bin/count.cgi?df=lmhobbs.dat">

The counter at Claranet also allows you to specify the type of counter and the width of the frame. They even allow you to display a clock with the current time or the date instead of a counter.

Hopefully your service provider will have clear instructions on their Web site, Claranet certainly do. Please also remember that the procedure for your service provider could be very different to the one shown here which is only for illustration purposes.

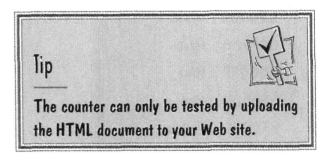

Tip

The counter can only be tested by uploading the HTML document to your Web site.

146

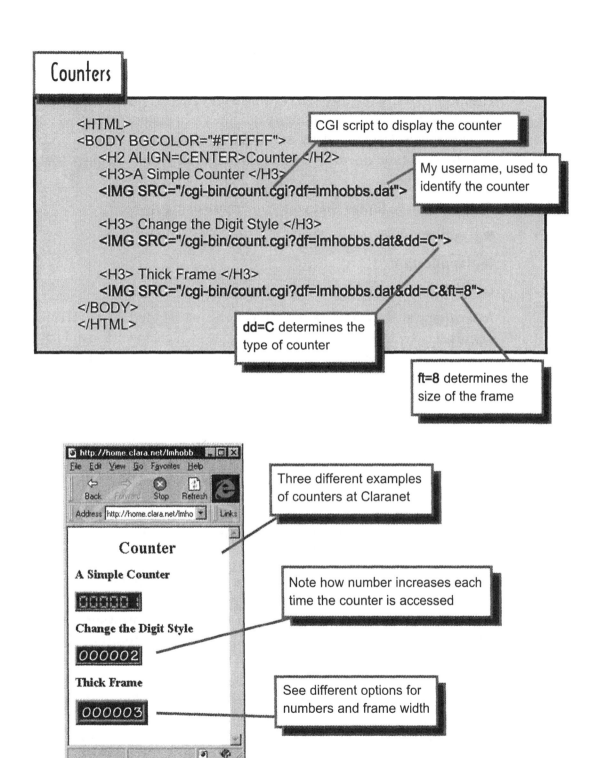

Counters

```
<HTML>
<BODY BGCOLOR="#FFFFFF">
    <H2 ALIGN=CENTER>Counter </H2>
    <H3>A Simple Counter </H3>
    <IMG SRC="/cgi-bin/count.cgi?df=lmhobbs.dat">

    <H3> Change the Digit Style </H3>
    <IMG SRC="/cgi-bin/count.cgi?df=lmhobbs.dat&dd=C">

    <H3> Thick Frame </H3>
    <IMG SRC="/cgi-bin/count.cgi?df=lmhobbs.dat&dd=C&ft=8">
</BODY>
</HTML>
```

CGI script to display the counter

My username, used to identify the counter

dd=C determines the type of counter

ft=8 determines the size of the frame

Three different examples of counters at Claranet

Note how number increases each time the counter is accessed

See different options for numbers and frame width

http://home.clara.net/lmhobb

File Edit View Go Favorites Help

Back Forward Stop Refresh

Address http://home.clara.net/lmho   Links

Counter

A Simple Counter

Change the Digit Style

000002

Thick Frame

000003

Java

The Internet has gone through revolutionary stages and the introduction of the Java language definitely qualifies as a major technological breakthrough. Developed by Sun Microsystems, Java turns a web page from a static document with minimal interaction to a page that can come alive.

There are three things that you can create using Java:

- applet
- application
- beans

A Java **applet** is a program that can be embedded in an HTML document. Typically they are small programs which download quickly and perform a specific task. On the next page we will see how to use an applet which sends a message across the screen, similar to the <MARQUEE> tag that we saw earlier. However, this applet presents a message that is far more sophisticated than the HTML tag.

A Java **application** is almost identical to a Java applet. It is a program, written in Java, the only difference is that it stands alone and does not require a browser to run it.

Java **beans** are new. Each bean performs a very limited function, but they can be linked together or linked into Java applets and applications to extend their functions.

You may be wondering why Java is becoming so popular. One of its very attractive features is that a Java program will run on any computer, provided they have a Java capable web browser. Unlike other programs which have to be compiled for the operating system on the computer where they will run. Therefore, once the program is written, it can run anywhere. Anyone who bought an Apple Mac computer will remember the days when some software was not available for that machine, but would be for Microsoft Windows. Now if Java had been available then, this would not have been a problem.

Another nice aspect to Java programs is that they don't require an special installation procedure and if they are updated, then you automatically receive the latest version, the next time you run the program when you load it from their web site.

It is impossible here to cover this subject in any depth, therefore it is highly recommended that if you want to learn more about this subject to refer to the books, *Java Made Simple* and *Javascript Made Simple* by P.K.McBride.

Over the next few pages we will see how Java applets can be embedded in an HTML document and how we can use Javascript.

This page from Citibank is using a Java applet in the bottom left corner to display current stock prices and you can even specify the stock prices it is to display. Applet like this, which take input from visitors, can be used to customise a page to their requirements.

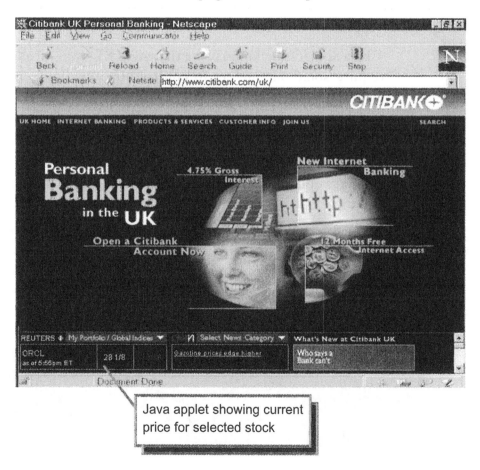

Java applet showing current price for selected stock

Java applet

Java applets appear on many web sites, performing a wide variety of tasks. There are many available, and non-programmer Web page designers would usually rather use an applet that has already been created. The following pages will concentrate on how to include an applet on our page.

There are many Java applets available on the Internet and some places that have a good library include:

- http://java.sun.com/applets/index.html
- http://www.developer.com/directories/pages/dir.java.html
- http://www.jars.com/
- http://javaboutique.internet.com/

Using a Java applet

A Java applet is included using the <APPLET> tag. All applets usually require some parameters to control how they look and what they display and don't be surprised if you have to specify many parameters.

The applet can be downloaded to your computer for testing, then stored with your other Web files on your ISP's computer. It can also be referenced from its home site on the Internet. When visitors arrive at a page containing an applet, its file will then be downloaded (from wherever it is held) to their comuter for running.

In the example shown below, taken from the Wolf 359 web site, they use an external Java applet to display a message. When we look at the HTML source above, we can see a parameter that points to an external web site and other parameters that specify the message, speed and size.

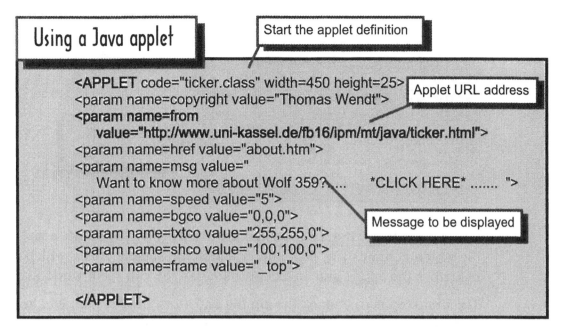

Using a Java applet

Start the applet definition

```
<APPLET code="ticker.class" width=450 height=25>
<param name=copyright value="Thomas Wendt">
<param name=from
    value="http://www.uni-kassel.de/fb16/ipm/mt/java/ticker.html">
<param name=href value="about.htm">
<param name=msg value="
    Want to know more about Wolf 359?...    *CLICK HERE* ....... ">
<param name=speed value="5">
<param name=bgco value="0,0,0">
<param name=txtco value="255,255,0">
<param name=shco value="100,100,0">
<param name=frame value="_top">

</APPLET>
```

Applet URL address

Message to be displayed

At the Java boutique web site (below), you can view many, many applets and see them in operation.

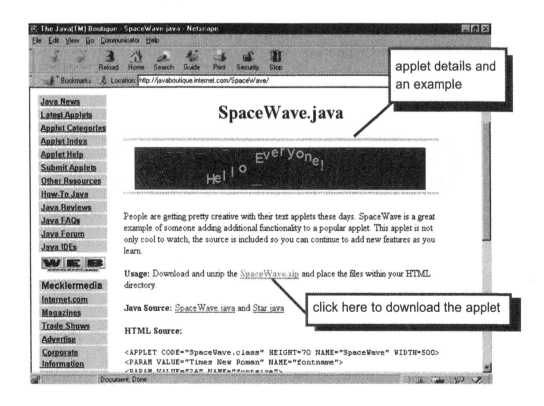

applet details and an example

click here to download the applet

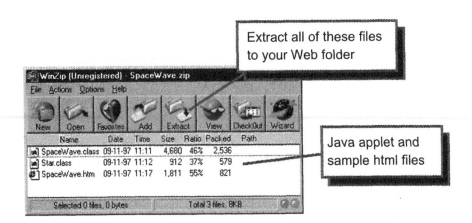

Extract all of these files to your Web folder

Java applet and sample html files

For each applet, all the required files are normally packaged into a zip file which contains the Java applet and some sample HTML which describes the applet and an example so that you can see it working.

The first step is to unpack the zip file and store the Java applets in your web directory. Then take the sample HTML and modify the parameters to suit your requirements.

All applets have a name and the applet is referenced using the **CODE=** clause inside the applet tag. You should not change the name because otherwise the browser won't be able to find the applet. Modify the parameters, following the style in the sample HTML, to suit your needs. In this example for SpaceWave we pass in parameters for the font, message, size and moving characteristics.

When the applet definition is complete, the **</APPLET>** tag terminates it. Now we can include any other HTML such as headings, tables etc. The Java applet can be tested using your browser without connecting to the Internet. When you are satisfied with the applet, you can then include the HTML in the document where the applet is to be used. Don't forget to include your Java applets when you upload your HTML files to your Web site.

When designing a page, always consider the time required to download and start the Java applet. Although they can have a stunning effect on a Web site, their value is nill is the reader will not wait for the applet to start. Another consideration is that not every browsers support Java so some readers will not be able to see your page.

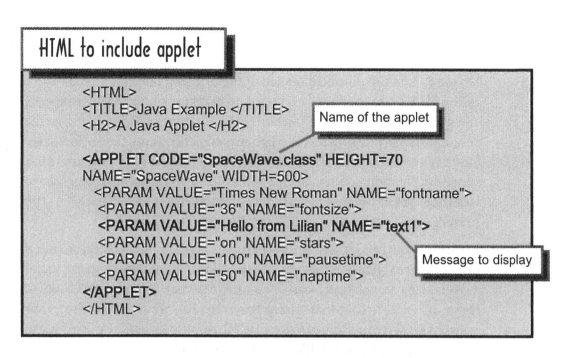

HTML to include applet

```
<HTML>
<TITLE>Java Example </TITLE>
<H2>A Java Applet </H2>

<APPLET CODE="SpaceWave.class" HEIGHT=70
NAME="SpaceWave" WIDTH=500>
  <PARAM VALUE="Times New Roman" NAME="fontname">
  <PARAM VALUE="36" NAME="fontsize">
  <PARAM VALUE="Hello from Lilian" NAME="text1">
  <PARAM VALUE="on" NAME="stars">
  <PARAM VALUE="100" NAME="pausetime">
  <PARAM VALUE="50" NAME="naptime">
</APPLET>
</HTML>
```

Name of the applet

Message to display

our Java applet

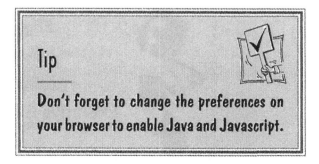

Tip

Don't forget to change the preferences on your browser to enable Java and Javascript.

153

Javascript

Netscape has developed Javascript, a scripting language that works within HTML. Javascript is included directly in your HTML document, using the **<SCRIPT>** tags. As the HTML is processed, the Javascript commands are interpreted and processed at the same time. However, in order to use Javascript, your visitor must be using a browser that supports it and has Javascript enabled. If you are not sure as to whether your browser supports Javascript then check in the *Preferences* section to see if it can be enabled/disabled.

Javascript, although not as powerful as Java, is frequently included on Web sites, because it is very easy to learn. Another benefit is that a Web site can contain many files and it is very easy to lose some of them, or forget to upload them to your site. With Javascript, your instructions are included in your HTML document so they are easy to manage and you are not likely to mislay them.

Javascript is becoming quite popular, for example, this page from British Airways makes extensive use of Javascript, including a scrolling message to bring to your attention the latest news.

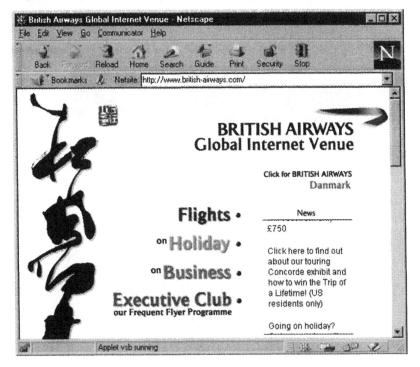

If you have ever written a program before then you should have no problem using Javascript because it has most of the attributes of any programming language, such as the ability to define variables, display messages, trap error conditions and loop for a certain period of time.

You can create your own functions which call Javascript functions, then to call any of these or the supplied functions, you call them, inside <SCRIPT> tags which are placed inside a <BODY> tag, as we can see in this example.

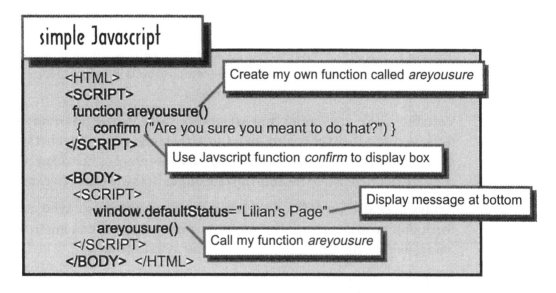

simple Javascript

```
<HTML>
<SCRIPT>
 function areyousure()
  {  confirm ("Are you sure you meant to do that?") }
</SCRIPT>

<BODY>
  <SCRIPT>
     window.defaultStatus="Lilian's Page"
     areyousure()
  </SCRIPT>
</BODY> </HTML>
```

Create my own function called *areyousure*

Use Javscript function *confirm* to display box

Display message at bottom

Call my function *areyousure*

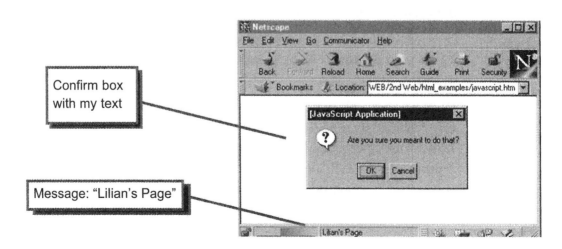

Confirm box with my text

Message: "Lilian's Page"

Some of the other useful functions include *onclick* for when you click a button, *onMouseOver* activates when mouse is dragged over this area and *alert* to create an message box.

To output information use the *write* function which generates HTML to send to the browser. Therefore this function is unusual because you have to say to yourself, what HTML do I need to generate the required output. For example, suppose you want two blank lines and then the text you would enter

```
document.write(" <BR> <BR> Text goes here ")
```

Programs usually need variables and in Javascript you can define numbers, strings, boolean values and null values. Remember that variables do not have to be static, they can be used in calculations and incremented or decremented in loops.

Variables are given names and assigned a value using the equal sign. If the variable is of type text, then the text string is specified between quotes. When referencing variables you must refer to them exactly as they are defined using the appropriate upper or lowercase characters.

Arrays may also be defined and then their contents displayed using for loops or other methods. An important point to remember with arrays is that the first position in the array is zero not 1

If you have ever wondered how a web page can receive some data, perform calculations and then redisplay it. They are most probably using Javascript to do that.

Javascript also contains a comprehensive set of commands to perform loops and perform conditional commands using if then else statements.

On these few pages we have just scratched the surface on what you can do in Javascript. A comprehensive list of Javascript functions and how to use them can be obtained from books like *Javascript Made Simple* by P.K.McBride or from the Netscape site at:

home.netscape.com/comprod/products/navigator/version_2.0/script/index.html

arrays and variables

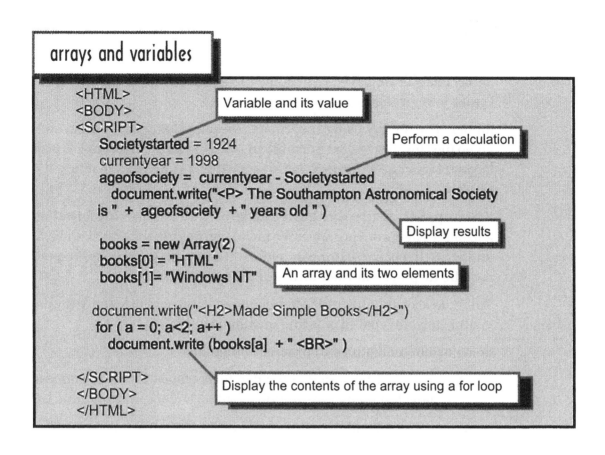

```
<HTML>
<BODY>
<SCRIPT>
    Societystarted = 1924
    currentyear = 1998
    ageofsociety =  currentyear - Societystarted
      document.write("<P> The Southampton Astronomical Society
    is " +  ageofsociety  + " years old " )


    books = new Array(2)
    books[0] = "HTML"
    books[1]= "Windows NT"

  document.write("<H2>Made Simple Books</H2>")
   for ( a = 0; a<2; a++ )
     document.write (books[a]  + " <BR>" )

</SCRIPT>
</BODY>
</HTML>
```

Variable and its value

Perform a calculation

Display results

An array and its two elements

Display the contents of the array using a for loop

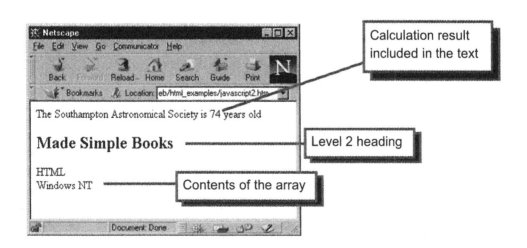

Calculation result included in the text

Level 2 heading

Contents of the array

Summary

In this chapter we have learnt some techniques that will enable us to create very professional looking web sites.

Rather than always using static data, we can also include sound and video files for the reader to download. Watching a preview clip of next weeks favourite TV episode is far more interesting than reading the synopsis.

If Java applets are used on the web page then even more customisation and fancy effects are possible. We have seen how a bank can use a Java applet so that each visitor can request the stocks they are interested in to be displayed at the bottom of the web page.

Using Javascript in your HTML document, you can interact with the visitor beyond what is possible in standard HTML.

Some useful techniques to practise would be:

❑   review from sound and video files, check their size and see how long they take to download;

❑   review the libraries of Java applets that are available on the Internet and select some and see you can customise them for your web page;

❑   investigate how you could modify your form document to use Javascript.

8 Housekeeping

Installing your Web page 160

Uploading with Netscape 162

Good housekeeping 163

Uploading with Internet Explorer . . 164

Opening your Web page 166

Home page 168

Telling the world 170

Meta 174

Space saving tips 176

Bringing it all together 177

Summary 178

Installing your Web page

The time has now come to install your Web pages on the Internet. The steps involved will depend on whether the pages are being loaded onto a corporate Web site, or onto a service providers computer. This involves copying all the files that make up your Web page, i.e. the HTML source files, graphics, Java applets, sound and video files to the specified location.

A corporate Web site will have specific directories where HTML documents are located. To include your files, you will have to discuss with the Web site administrator, how and when you can do this. Amendment to the corporate home page may also be required, which could delay the availability of your Web pages.

If your Web pages are to be published via an Internet service provider, then they will advise the format and directories where your Web documents should be placed. The following text assumes that your files are to be published via a service provider. There are several ways that these files can be transferred:

- Using the utility FTP;
- Netscape Composer;
- Internet Explorer.

The **FTP** utility is perfect for copying files to the service provider's computer. When using this utility, you should to set the file type — use ASCII for HTML text files, and binary for sound, graphics and video files. You can select one or many files to transfer.

Once the primary HTML document is renamed to the format specified by your Internet provider, your pages will be visible on the Internet, e.g. at Claranet, the main HTML document must be called *index.html*.

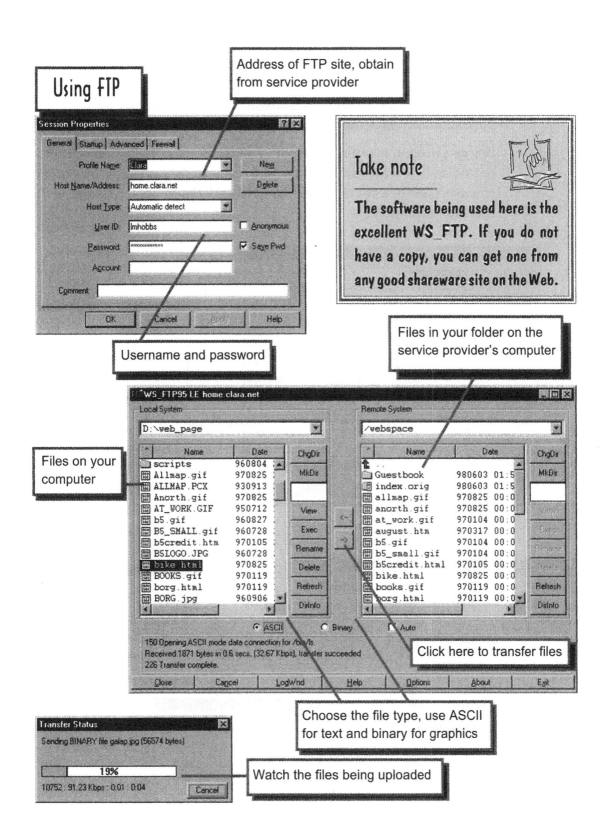

Using FTP

Address of FTP site, obtain from service provider

Session Properties

General | Startup | Advanced | Firewall

Profile Name: Clara

Host Name/Address: home.clara.net

Host Type: Automatic detect

User ID: lmhobbs

Password: ***********

Account:

Comment:

New

Delete

Anonymous

Save Pwd

OK | Cancel | Apply | Help

Username and password

Take note

The software being used here is the excellent WS_FTP. If you do not have a copy, you can get one from any good shareware site on the Web.

Files in your folder on the service provider's computer

WS_FTP95 LE home.clara.net

Local System

D:\web_page

Files on your computer

Name	Date	
scripts	960804	
Allmap.gif	970825	
ALLMAP.PCX	930913	
Anorth.gif	970825	
AT_WORK.GIF	950712	
b5.gif	960827	
B5_SMALL.gif	960728	
b5credit.htm	970105	
B5LOGO.JPG	960728	
bike.html	970825	
BOOKS.gif	970119	
borg.html	970119	
BORG.jpg	960906	

ChgDir
MkDir

View
Exec
Rename
Delete
Refresh
DirInfo

Remote System

/webspace

Name	Date	
. .		
Guestbook	980603	01:5
index.orig	980603	01:5
allmap.gif	970825	00:0
anorth.gif	970825	00:0
at_work.gif	970104	00:0
august.htm	970317	00:0
b5.gif	970104	00:0
b5_small.gif	970104	00:0
b5credit.html	970105	00:0
bike.html	970825	00:0
books.gif	970119	00:0
borg.html	970119	00:0

ChgDir
MkDir

View
Exec
Rename
Delete
Refresh
DirInfo

ASCII   Binary   Auto

150 Opening ASCII mode data connection for /bin/ls.
Received 1871 bytes in 0.6 secs. (32.67 Kbps), transfer succeeded
226 Transfer complete.

Close | Cancel | LogWnd | Help | Options | About | Exit

Click here to transfer files

Choose the file type, use ASCII for text and binary for graphics

Transfer Status

Sending BINARY file galap.jpg (56574 bytes)

19%

10752 : 91.23 Kbps : 0:01 0:04   Cancel

Watch the files being uploaded

161

Uploading with Netscape

Alternatively, the Composer software in Netscape can be used to publish your pages onto the Internet.

Before you can use this to upload, you must connect to your service provider. Then fill in the boxes shown here, to specify the files to transfer and then click on the OK button. All the specified files will be loaded automatically.

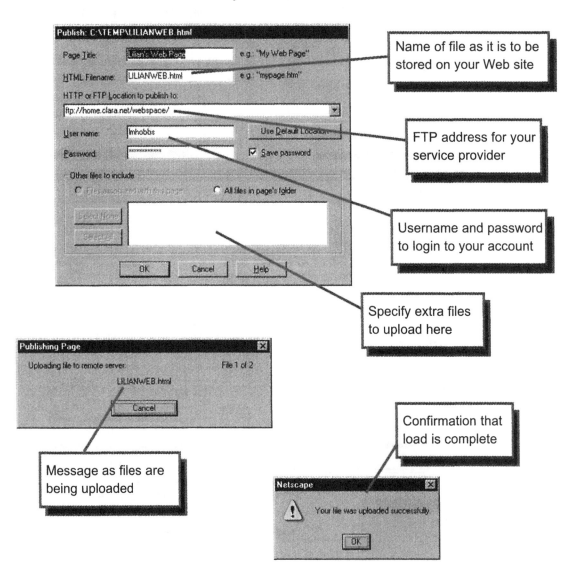

Name of file as it is to be stored on your Web site

FTP address for your service provider

Username and password to login to your account

Specify extra files to upload here

Message as files are being uploaded

Confirmation that load is complete

Good housekeeping

When constructing Web documents it is very important to adopt good housekeeping practices. A personal Web site, hosted by an Internet service provider will not backup your Web page, therefore it is up to you to make sure that they are safe. Good housekeeping means:

- Keep all your Web files together in the same folder e.g. the author uses d:\web_page.

- Copy all the files to a floppy disk as a backup or use Microsoft Backup to make a copy of the files.

- Always create a new backup floppy disk when you change your Web page.

- Label the floppy disks with the date the Web page was constructed.

- When you install the Web page on your Internet service provider's computer, always rename the files that you are about to replace, so that you have a local backup copy. Then install the new files. Fail to do so and if you make a mistake you could lose the original version of your Web site and have nothing to fall back to.

- If your files are large, use a compression utility like PKZIP to store the files on your local disk.

- Use the comment feature to specify a version of the file and the date that you last changed it.

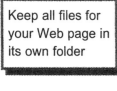

Keep all files for your Web page in its own folder

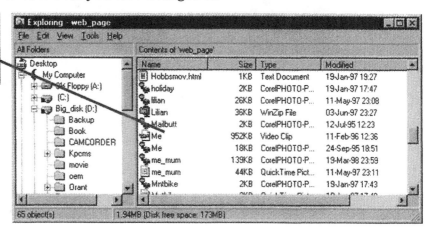

Uploading with Internet Explorer

Users of Internet Explorer 4, can publish their Web pages using the provided utility, **Web Publishing wizard**. Since this is a wizard, and it seems that all wizards must ask quite a lot of questions, you will find that there is far more work to do when using this tool.

One point to bear in mind is that it will try to connect to your service provider and then prompt you for your username and password to logon, so be ready.

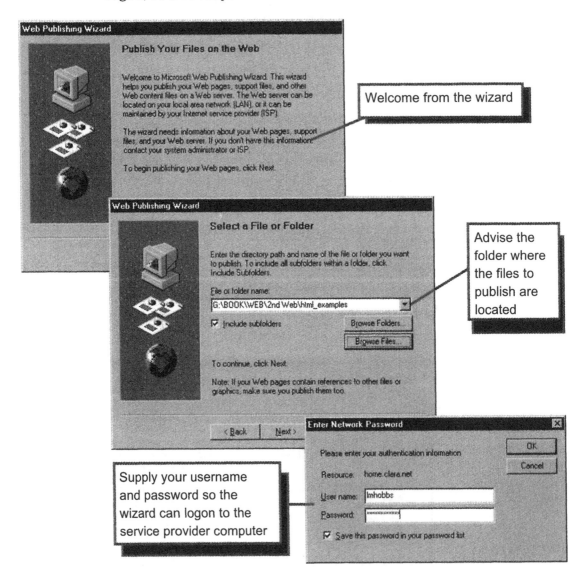

Welcome from the wizard

Advise the folder where the files to publish are located

Supply your username and password so the wizard can logon to the service provider computer

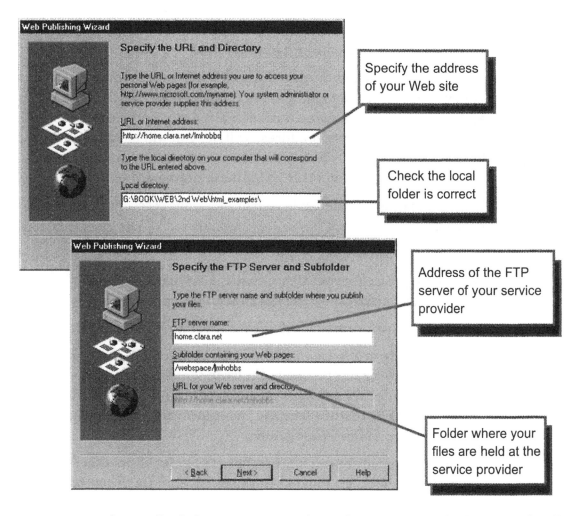

Specify the URL and Directory

Type the URL or Internet address you use to access your personal Web pages (for example, http://www.microsoft.com/myname). Your system administrator or service provider supplies this address.

URL or Internet address:
http://home.clara.net/lmhobbs

Type the local directory on your computer that will correspond to the URL entered above.

Local directory:
G:\BOOK\WEB\2nd Web\html_examples\

Specify the address of your Web site

Check the local folder is correct

Specify the FTP Server and Subfolder

Type the FTP server name and subfolder where you publish your files.

FTP server name:
home.clara.net

Subfolder containing your Web pages:
/webspace/lmhobbs

URL for your Web server and directory:
http://home.clara.net/lmhobbs

Address of the FTP server of your service provider

Folder where your files are held at the service provider

< Back   Next >   Cancel   Help

Once all of these questions have been answered, the wizard will connect to your service provider and upload all of the files. With an insight into how you can transfer files using Internet Explorer and Netscape, you may decide to use FTP which is in fact what these tools are doing behind the scenes.

No matter which approach you use, you will not be able to upload any files unless you know the address and your username and password to logon. Of course, if you forget your username and password you cannot even connect to your service provider. But if the details are stored in an automatic connection it is easy to forget what they are!

165

Opening your Web page

Once all of your files have been published on the Internet, it's time to see how the page looks to the whole world.

A Web page is invoked by entering its address, also known as a URL. Today it is very common to see companies including their Web address on advertising material, such as http://www.oracle.com. As to what your own Internet address will be, you will have to ask your Internet provider or Web administrator, to advise on their naming scheme. e.g. the author's is http://home.clara.net/lmhobbs

When you specify this address in your browser, one of several things could happen:

● the page displays;

● the page displays but the format is not what you required. Edit the page, upload it to the Internet and try again;

● A URL error occurs, which means it cannot find your page.

Some of these problems could be caused by the HTML documents or files being stored using filenames the wrong case, e.g. some computers would consider the files a.htm and A.HTM to be different. Another reason could be that the files have been stored using the wrong name or even stored in the wrong folder.

If your home page doesn't appear then try to invoke another page by calling it directly, e.g. to invoke the page sas.html at the author's Web site you would specify

http://home.clara.net/lmhobbs/sas.html

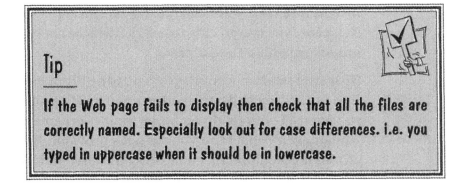

Tip

If the Web page fails to display then check that all the files are correctly named. Especially look out for case differences. i.e. you typed in uppercase when it should be in lowercase.

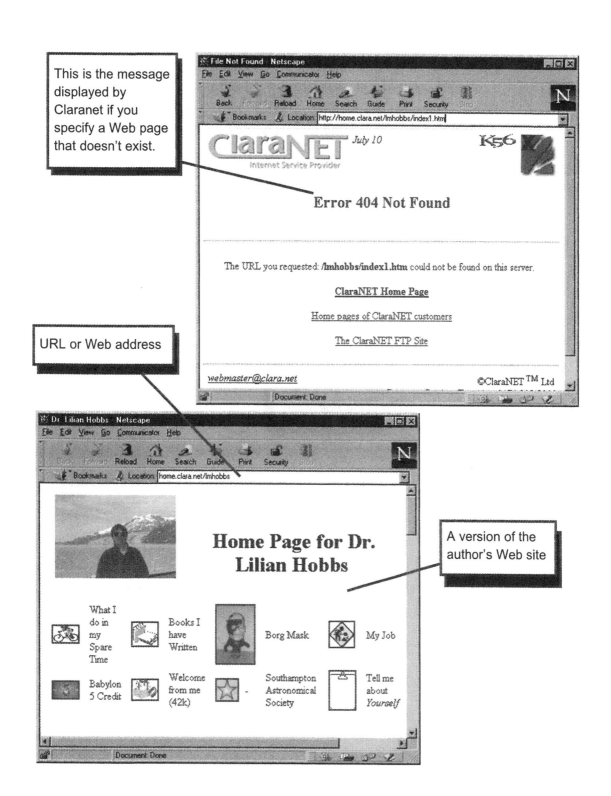

This is the message displayed by Claranet if you specify a Web page that doesn't exist.

File Not Found - Netscape

File Edit View Go Communicator Help

Back Forward Reload Home Search Guide Print Security Stop

Bookmarks & Location: http://home.clara.net/lmhobbs/index1.htm

ClaraNET *July 10*
Internet Service Provider

K56

Error 404 Not Found

The URL you requested: **/lmhobbs/index1.htm** could not be found on this server.

ClaraNET Home Page

Home pages of ClaraNET customers

The ClaraNET FTP Site

webmaster@clara.net

©ClaraNET ™ Ltd

Document Done

URL or Web address

Dr. Lilian Hobbs - Netscape

File Edit View Go Communicator Help

Back Forward Reload Home Search Guide Print Security Stop

Bookmarks & Location: home.clara.net/lmhobbs

Home Page for Dr. Lilian Hobbs

A version of the author's Web site

What I do in my Spare Time

Books I have Written

Borg Mask

My Job

Babylon 5 Credit

Welcome from me (42k)

Southampton Astronomical Society

Tell me about *Yourself*

Document Done

Home page

Once your pages are installed on your Web site, you can customise your browser so that every time it is launched or you click on the **Home** icon 🏠, your Web page is displayed automatically. The technique for customising will vary for each browser.

Netscape

It is not immediately obvious with Netscape where to find the home page information. You have to select *Edit* from the strip menu and then select *Preferences*. When the window is displayed the middle box should be the one where you can enter the address of your home page. If it isn't, then click on *Navigator* in the *Category* section. Then to make your Web page the default, enter its address into the location box in the **Home Page** section. If you can't remember the name of the file then click on the *Browse* button.

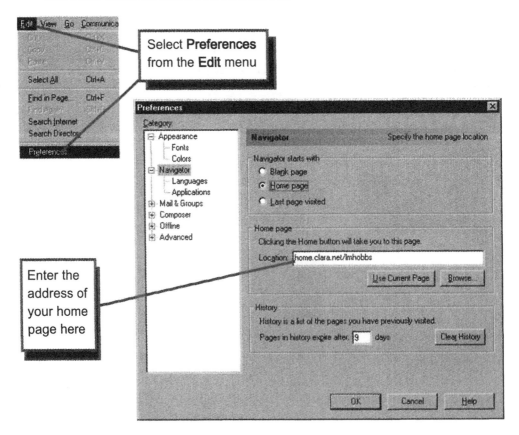

Select **Preferences** from the **Edit** menu

Enter the address of your home page here

Internet Explorer

Start by selecting *Options* from the *View* menu, then click on the *Navigation* tab. Take care here, because Internet Explorer allows you to specify the addresses of a number of pages. Therefore make sure that you have selected **Start Page** (Explorer's term for the home page) from the drop-down list for Page. Then enter the address of your home page into the *address* box. Click on the *OK* button and your browser preferences will be updated.

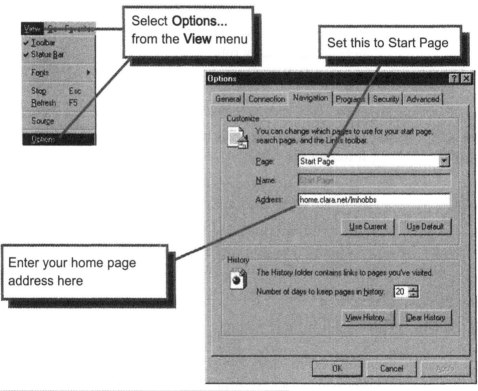

Select **Options...** from the **View** menu

Set this to Start Page

Enter your home page address here

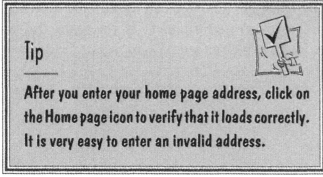

Tip

After you enter your home page address, click on the Home page icon to verify that it loads correctly. It is very easy to enter an invalid address.

Telling the world

Once your Web pages are installed, you will want to tell the world that they are there. Here are some reasons why you should announce your Web site:

- for the benefit of friends or relatives who have lost touch and may be trying to find you;
- you run a club and somebody needs some information;
- to sell or promote your product;
- your site includes information that may be of interest to people, say hobby related or pertains to a TV show;
- for family tree researchers;

There are several ways you can let people know about your site:

- include your WWW address on all correspondence, such as letters and e-mail.
- register your pages with search engines like Altavista, Yahoo and Infoseek, so your Web page is included in their database

Trying to find information on the Internet is not always easy. People searching for information use Internet search engines which have databases of what is held on Web pages. They are updated regularly and there is no charge to include a reference to your Web site.

AltaVista http://www.altavista.com

Altavista is one of the most popular search engines and has grown to be one of the largest, with computers around the globe. If you visit the main site www.altavista.com, then you can find a local AltaVista site and use that for improved performance. If you want the widest possible audience for your Web site, it pays to register with Altavista.

Adding your URL

At the main Altavista page, click on the **Add/Remove** URL option. You are then prompted to enter your URL, it's that simple.

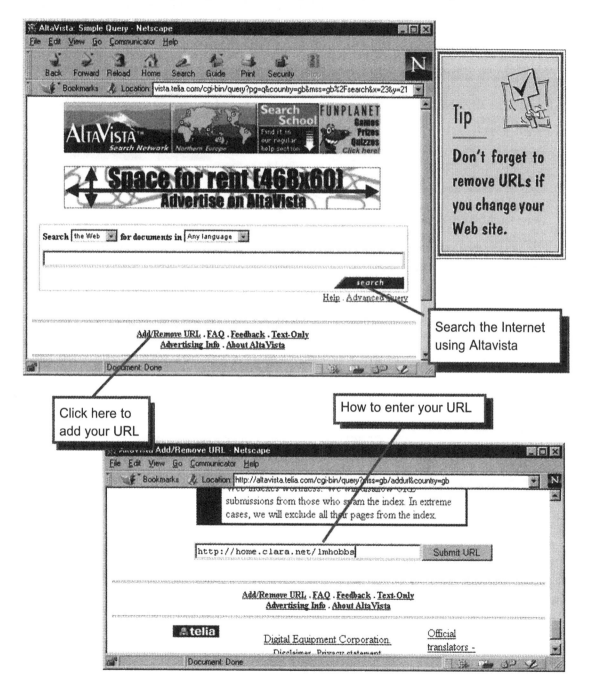

Search the Internet using Altavista

Click here to add your URL

How to enter your URL

Tip

Don't forget to remove URLs if you change your Web site.

Yahoo http://www.yahoo.com

Another popular search engine is Yahoo. The approach that you have to use to register your site here is rather different. You have to select the category where your Web page belongs and then click on *'How to Suggest a Web Site'*. Yahoo makes you fill in a number of screens before your entry is added to their database.

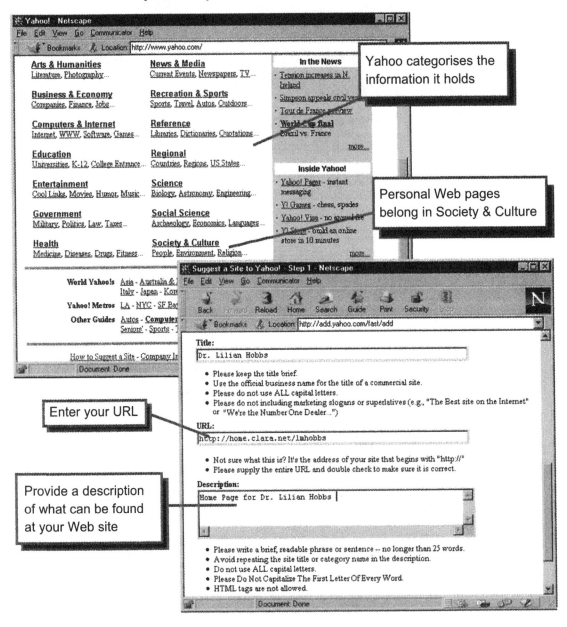

Infoseek http://www.infoseek.com

Infoseek, like Altavista, makes it very easy for you to add your URL to their database. Just click on the **Add URL** option and you are presented with guidelines about how to register. Then you fill in the box with your URL entry and your site will be included in the database. What these search engines tend to do is look at the first part of your Web page and then use that as the description for your Web site.

Another nice feature available at Infoseek is that you can check on the status of your submission. If you see that it has been processed, you can verify this by doing a search on Infoseek using your details.

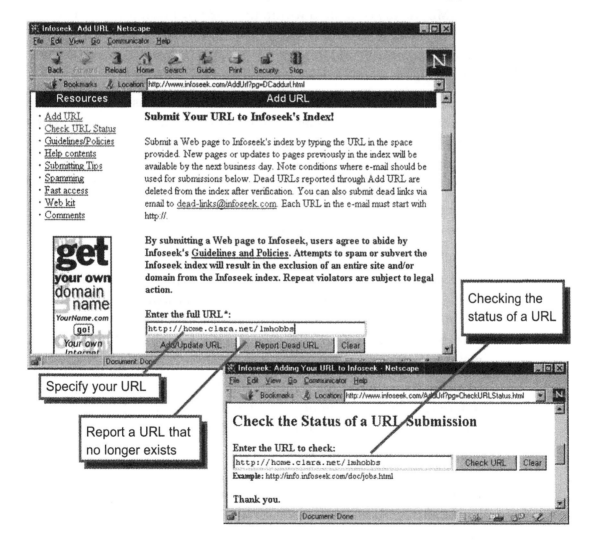

Meta

When a search engine is asked to register your Web page in its database, it searches your Web page for information to include. In the past, that has mean that important information could be overlooked and trivial information included. The solution to this problem is to use the <META> tag which tells the Internet search engine what is to be indexed. Other information can be specified inside the <META> tag, but we will concentrate on its indexing features.

<META>

The **<META>** tag is defined within the **<HEAD>** tag and can be used in two ways to index our Web page. The first format is using the clauses **Name= "keywords"** and **Content= " "**. This is the one to use to tell the search engine which words it should index.

The word *keywords* is placed inside the **Name=** clause to advise that keywords are being supplied. Then inside the **Content=** clause, write every keyword that is to be associated with this Web document. You may specify as many words or phrases as you like, each one is separated by a comma.

Therefore, entries that could be specified for the author's Web page is the author's name, "Lilian Hobbs" and the word "author".

        <META NAME="keywords" CONTENT=" Lilian Hobbs, author" >

Once the search engine has scanned this Web page, these two entries are put into its database. If you were to query using a search engine like Altavista, and you entered the word "author" as part of your search parameters, then this page should be returned in the list of matching entries.

By using the <META> tag it allows you to reference your page many different ways. For example, if you view the source of the AA's Web page, one of their index entries is "Yellow Van".

You may specify as many entries as you like for the content. If they will not all fit on one line, then start a new line, remembering to terminate the line with a comma as illustrated in the following example.

```
<META NAME="keywords"
CONTENT=" Lilian Hobbs, author, Oracle, Rdb, Home Page book,
Bike book, Astronomy, Southampton Astronomical Society,
Babylon 5 " >
```

When a search engine selects your page, it normally displays the first few lines of text that it finds on your Web page. Depending on the pages content, this may not convey much to the reader. This problem can be overcome by using the clause **Name= "description",** because it tells the search engine to display the text found within the **content=** clause, as shown below.

```
<META NAME="description"
CONTENT=" Lilian is the author of two Made Simple books" >
```

Therefore, if you searched in Altavista using the name Lilian Hobbs, after your Web page URL it would display the following description. When a <META> tag is used on your Web page, it does not appear when the document is displayed, you can only see the values when you ask for the HTML source to be displayed.

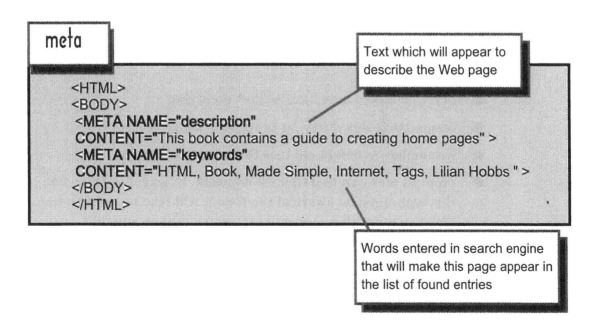

meta

```
<HTML>
<BODY>
<META NAME="description"
CONTENT="This book contains a guide to creating home pages" >
<META NAME="keywords"
CONTENT="HTML, Book, Made Simple, Internet, Tags, Lilian Hobbs " >
</BODY>
</HTML>
```

Text which will appear to describe the Web page

Words entered in search engine that will make this page appear in the list of found entries

Space saving tips

Most Internet providers limit the amount of space you can use for a Web page, although this amount has been increasing over the years. The first service provider that the author used only allowed about 100k. This wasn't very much and it was difficult to include any graphics. Now all that has changed and the author's current service provider Claranet, offers a staggering 25Mb of personal Web space. You may very well wonder how anyone could use up 25Mb, but it is very easy to consume it when you start storing graphics and especially video files.

However you can you keep the space used to a minimum by following some of these approaches:

- Use text rather than graphics;

- Use small graphic files;

- Use JPEG instead of GIF files;

- Don't use too many graphic files;

- Ensure graphic files are their smallest size. You can decrease the size by saving as fewer colours or making the image smaller;

- Use graphics from a library provided by your Internet service provider;

- Don't include movie files or limit their use;

- Avoid using sound files or keep them small in size;

- Remember to delete old files that are no longer required;

- Point to files external to your Web site. However, when using this technique be aware of the time it will take to retrieve the file. You must also remember to respect other people's copyright. If you want to include someone else's images in your page, you must have their permission.

Bringing it all together

Now that we have seen many of the techniques that you can use to build a Web page. How do you create one of those nice-looking pages that you have seen?

Many commercial sites are created and maintained by professional Web page designers, some of whom were graphic artists. To create some of the impressive graphics with different types of images then you will probably need access to professional graphic software such as that from Adobe. However, these tools are not essential and with tools like Paint Shop Pro you can create good quality images.

All the examples in this book have been simple ones. All you need to do now is to combine these techniques together to create the desired effect. For instance, that could mean creating an image map for navigating the site, using frames to separate the navigation area from the text area, using a table to include your company logo with some text and creating the sites with multiple documents and plenty of links to other Web sites containing relevant information.

A Web page is an evolving document and often it pays to start with something simple and then improve upon your design. Spend some time looking at other Web sites to gather ideas on presentation and content. Don't be afraid to try new techniques and experiment. Remember that you can work on the Web page without being connected to the Internet. Therefore you only have to publish it when you are ready. Alternatively, you could publish it, but not place it in a location where it is easily accessible and then ask people to review its content before moving your Web page to a public place.

Finally, a Web page doesn't have to include fancy graphics. Simple text presented with a nice background and external links may not win you any awards, but it will be fast and informative.

Summary

In this final chapter we have seen how we can upload our documents to the Internet, which isn't very difficult and there are some tools around to make this job easier.

Once our page is on the Internet, it is nice if people can find it and therefore its worth spending a little time registering your page with the main search engines and using the <META> tags to ensure that your page is indexed so that users can locate it.

Finally, now that you have a Web page, do keep all the files that comprise your page, such as graphics, HTML and Java applets in a safe place. Your Internet provider will not back them up and you would be very disappointed if they were lost.

Hopefully you will agree that creating a Web page is not that difficult and the HTML language is quite easy to learn.

Index

Symbols

.htm 12
.html 12
<!-> 42
<A > 98
<A HREF=> 98, 100, 102, 125, 139, 143
<A NAME= 98
<A> 139, 143
<ADDRESS> 36
<APPLET> 150
<AREA>, image maps 107
<B> 32
<BGSOUND> 140
<BLINK> 34
<BLOCKQUOTE> 40, 41
<BODY BACKGROUND 93
<BODY> 13, 52, 93

 30, 31
<CAPTION> 66
<CITE> 34
<DL> 54
<EM> 32
<EMBED> 140
<FONT SIZE=> 50
<FONT> 50
<FORM> 126
<FRAME> 116
<FRAMESET> 116
<H...> 14, 28
<HEAD> 12
<HR> 60
<HTML> 12, 14
<I> 32
<IMG> 80, 107, 147
<INPUT NAME=> 126
<INPUT> 126, 130
<LH> 54
<LI> 53, 54
<LINK> 111
<MAP> 107
<MARQUEE> 144
<META> 174
<NOFRAME> 117
<OL> 54
<OPTION> 130

<P> 30
<PRE> 40
<Q> 34
<SAMP> 34
<SCRIPT> 154
<SELECT> 130
<STRONG> 32
<STYLE> 73
<SUB> 34
<SUP> 34
<TABLE> 64
<TD> 64
<TEXT AREA> 128
<TH> 66
<TITLE> 24
<TR> 64, 66
<U> 32
<UL> 54

A

ACTION= 126, 130
Address 36, 166
ALIGN= 38, 60, 68, 80
Alt= ,IMG option 84
AltaVista 170
Angle brackets 4

B

Background 93
  colour 73
  image 73
  sound 140
Backup 163
BEHAVIOR= 144
BGCOLOR= 52, 144
Bgcolor= 52
Blinking 34
Bold 32
Bookmark 24
Border = , table 66

C

CELLPADDING= 66
CELLSPACING= 66
CENTER 38
CGI 130, 147

Checkbox 130
Claranet 176
Color= 52
   <FONT> option 50
Colour 50, 52
COLS= 116
COLSPAN= 66
Column heading, Table 66
COLUMNS= 128
Comments 42
Composer 20, 44
COORD=, image maps 107
CorelDraw 95
Counter 146

D

Definition List 54, 57
Design, Web page 10
Digital cameras 87
DIRECTION= 144

E

Editors 20
Email 125

F

Face=, <FONT> option 50
File formats 79
Font 50
   colour 50, 73
   face 50
   size 50, 73
Form 8, 10, 124, 144, 148, 150, 154
   checkbox 130
   drop down list 130
   limit on fields 130
   tab control 128
   text area 128
   value limits 130
Forward-slash 12
Frame 8, 114
   change size 122
   margins 122
   NAME= 116
   nested 122
   resize 122

   scrolling 122
   simple 116
   SRC= 116
   targets 120
FrontPage Express 20, 46
   and graphics 92
   Tables 72

G

GIF 79
   89a Interlaced 86
Graphic 7, 78, 80
   align 80
   alternative text 84
   fast display 86
   in a table 88
   include 80
   jumps 104
   source 80
   space around it 82
   transparent 85
Graphic file formats 79

H

Headings 14, 28
HEIGHT= 82, 144
Highlighting text 32
Home page 2, 168
Horizontal ruler 60
Housekeeping 163
HREF= 98, 100, 107, 120, 125, 139, 143
HSPACE= 82
HTML 4
   document 12
   source 18
   start of document 14
HTML editors 20
Hyperlinks 98, 120
Hypertext 102

I

Image, transparent 85
Image maps 102, 106
   coordinates 107
   mapedit 109
Infoseek 173

Installing Web page 160
Interlaced GIF 86
Internet Explorer 169
   publishing documents 164
   Table options 68
Internet search engines, add URL 170
ISMAP 107
Italic 32

J

Java 148, 150
Javascript 154
JPEG 79
Jumping 98
   to another page 102
   using a graphic 104
JUSTIFY 38

K

Kodak Photo CD 87

L

LEFT 38
Level, headings 28
Limits, form entry 130
Lines 60
Linking 102
List 53
   bullet 73
   definition 54
   entry 54
   form 130
   numbered 54
   skip= 54
   unnumbered 54
LOOP= 140, 144

M

Mailto: 125
Mapedit 109
Margin 75, 122
MARGINHEIGHT= 122
MARGINWIDTH= 122
MAX= 130
Message, scroll across the screen 144
METHOD= 126
Microsoft Internet Explorer 3

MIN= 130
Multiple Pages 100

N

NAME= 98, 116, 128, 130
Nested frame 122
Nested list 58
Netscape Composer 44
   and graphics 91
   Tables 70
Netscape Navigator 3
New line 30
Nickname 24
NORESIZE 122
NOSHADE, HR option 60

O

Opening, Web page 166
Ordered List 56

P

Paint Shop Pro 79, 86
Paragraph 30
Photographs 87
Preformatted text 40

Q

Quicktime 142
Quotation 34

R

Real Audio 136
RIGHT 38
ROWS= 116, 128
ROWSPAN= 66
RULES= 68

S

Sample 34
Scanners 87
SCROLLAMOUNT= 144
Scrolling message 122, 144
SHAPE=, image maps 107
Simple table 64
SIZE= 60, 126, 130
   <FONT> option 50
Skip= 54

Sound
  add to web page 138, 140
  background 140
  Real Audio 136
  WAV files 136
Sound Recorder 138
Soundblaster 137
Source files, viewing 18
Space saving 176
Span, table multiple columns 66
Spelling 45
SRC= 80, 116, 140, 147
Style Sheet 73
  default 111
  link to 111
Subscript 34
Superscript 34

T

Tab, on a form 128
TABINDEX= 128
Table 62
  border 64, 66
  column data 66
  column headings 66
  column vertical alignment 68
  column width 66
  display cell options 68
  formatting 68
  heading 66
  including graphics 88
  line 66
  span multiple columns 66
  width 66
Tags 4
Target= 120
Text
  alignment 73
  blinking 34
  bold 32
  colour 52, 73
  font 73
  highlighting 32
  on a form 128
  paragraph 30

  preformatted 40
  quotation 34
  sample 34
  subscript 34
  superscript 34
  underline 32
Text=, colour option 52
TIFF 79
Title 24
Transparent images 85
TYPE= 128
TYPE=CHECKBOX 130
TYPE=RANGE 130

U

Underline 32
Uploading files 162
URL 2, 166
USEMAP= 107

V

VALIGN= 68
VALUE= 130
Vertical alignment, table column 68
Video 142
Viewing, Web page 16
VSPACE= 82

W

WAV 136
Web 2
Web browser 3
Web page
  design 10
  installing 160
  opening 166
  personal 10
  viewing 16
Web Publishing wizard 164
WIDTH= 60, 66, 68, 82, 144
Wingif 79
World Wide Web 2
WYSIWYG 44

Y

Yahoo 172

182